Maurer Rose Abstraction Challenge
Math Art Coloring Book

Dr Tanzelle Oberholster

aRtVerse

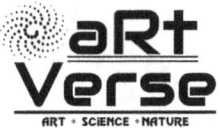

Copyright © 2020 Dr Tanzelle Oberholster

All rights reserved

No part of this book may be reproduced, or stored in a retrieval system, or transmitted in any form or by any means, electronic, mechanical, photocopying, recording, or otherwise, without express written permission of the publisher.

ISBN-13: 9798564420259

Cover design by: Dr Tanzelle Oberholster

CONTENTS

Title Page
Copyright
Introduction
About The Author 102

INTRODUCTION

The *Maurer Rose Abstraction Challenge: Math Art Coloring Book* contains 50 abstract geometric shapes generated through the R programming language for you to color. Each Maurer Rose was coded by me from scratch with unique mathematical parameters to create intricate, interlocking patterns inside.

The book features several polygons with 1 to 16 singular or duplicated points depending on whether an even or odd number was used. Even numbers have a duplicated number of polygon points, whereas odd numbers have singular points. The book includes maurer roses as circles (i.e., 1 angle or monogon), digons (2), triangles (3, trigon), squares (4, tetragon), pentagons (5), hexagons (6), heptagons (7), octagons (8), nonagons (9), decagons (10), hendecagons (11), dodecagons (12), tridecagons (13), tetradecagons (14), pentadecagon (15) and hexadecagon (16).

The maurer roses chosen for coloring have different complexity of their patterns and thus some may be easier to color whereas other are more challenging. The maurer roses are ideal to combine with color palettes in repeating blocks of color for maximum challenge and aesthetic impact! Additionally, there is space around each maurer rose for you to draw, doodle and tangle your own contributions!

I hope this provides you with an escape from the business of the world outside by challenging your creative skills!

Dr T Oberholster
Data Scientist (PhD Biotechnology)

Generative art includes designs generated by an autonomous system. Generative artists are also called algorists.

For more of my data adventures and math artwork, kindly visit me at aRtVerse!

art-verse.com

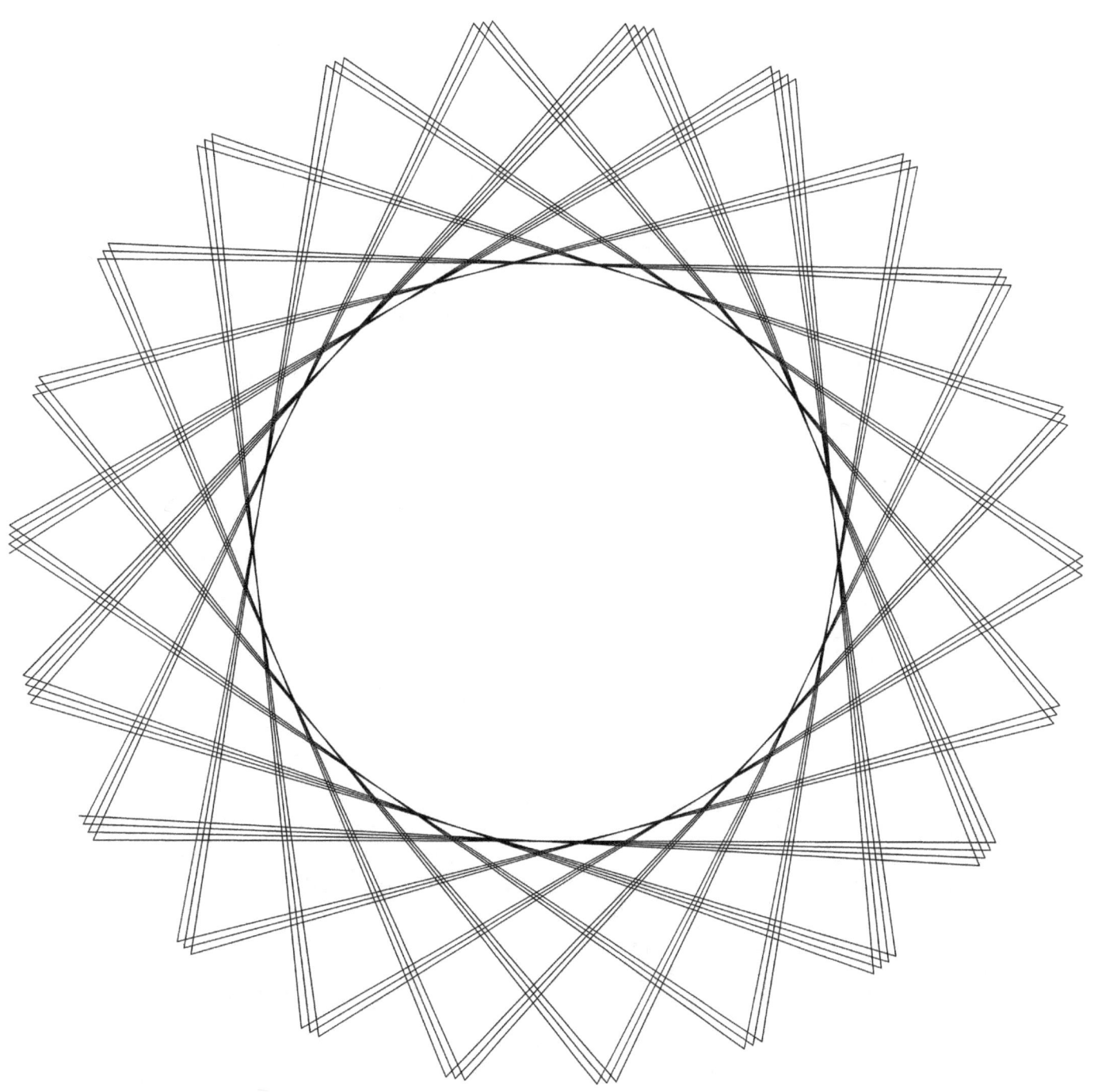

For more of my data adventures and math artwork, kindly visit me at aRtVerse (art-verse.com)!

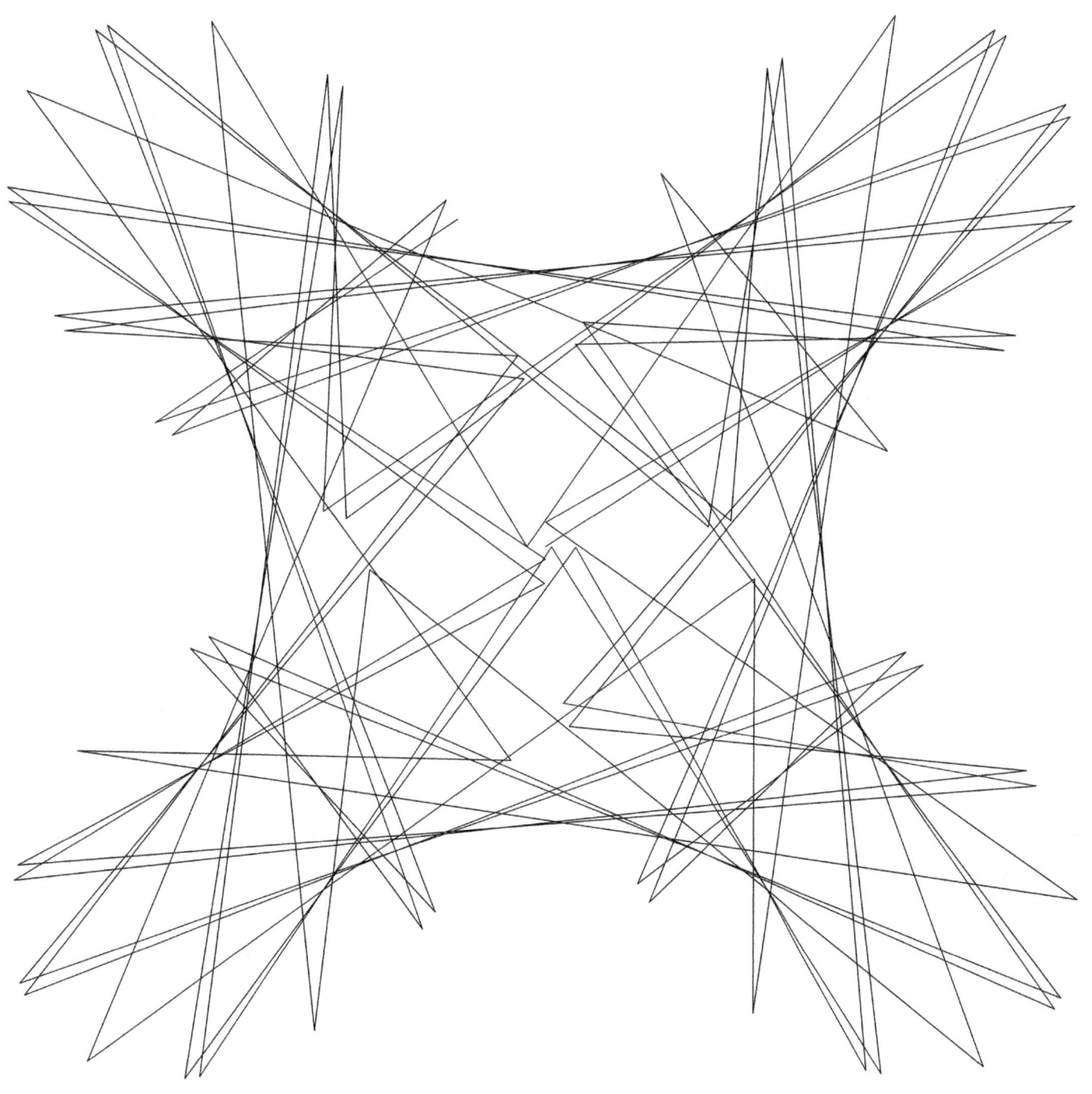

For more of my data adventures and math artwork, kindly visit me at aRtVerse (art-verse.com)!

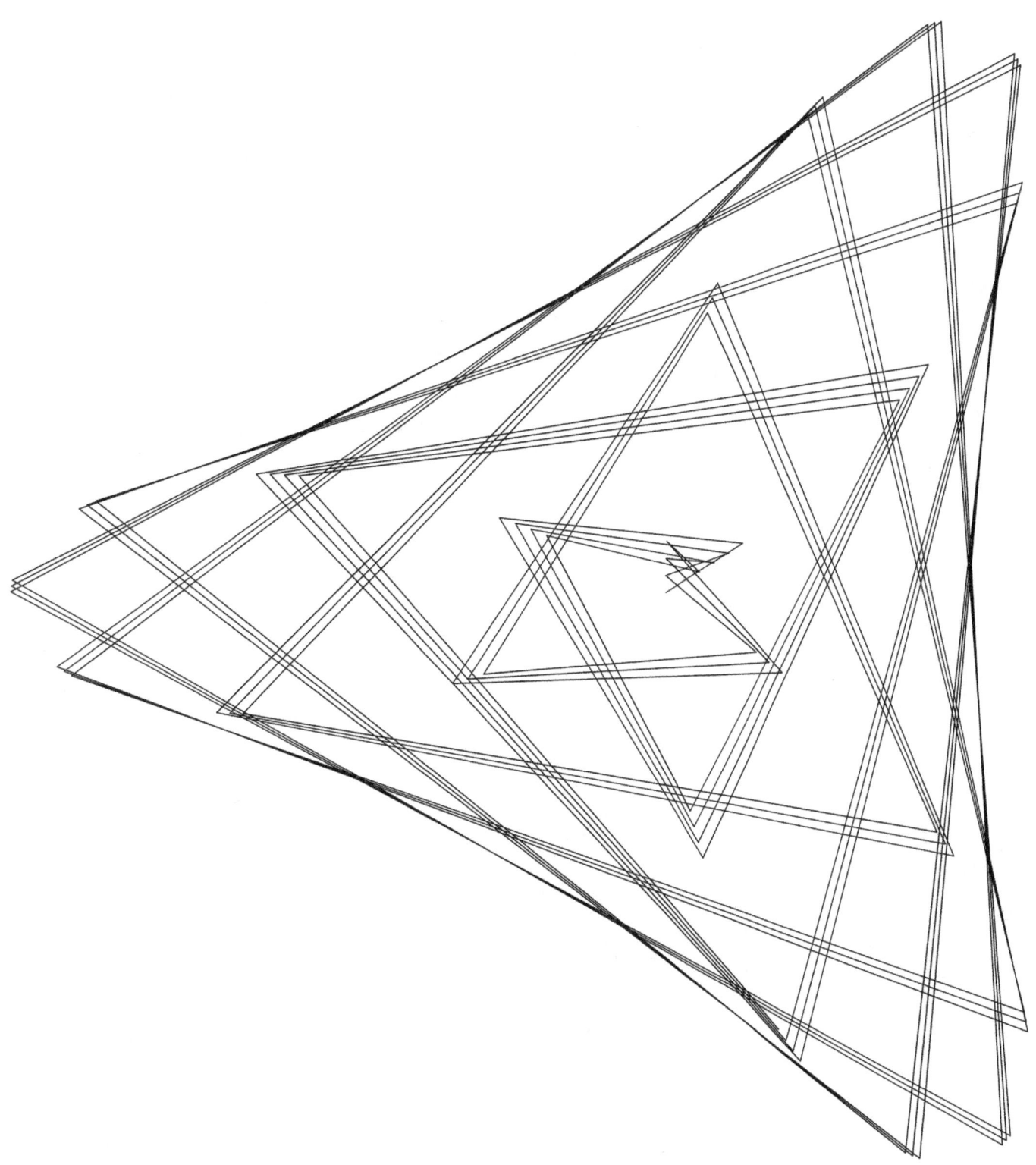

For more of my data adventures and math artwork, kindly visit me at aRtVerse (art-verse.com)!

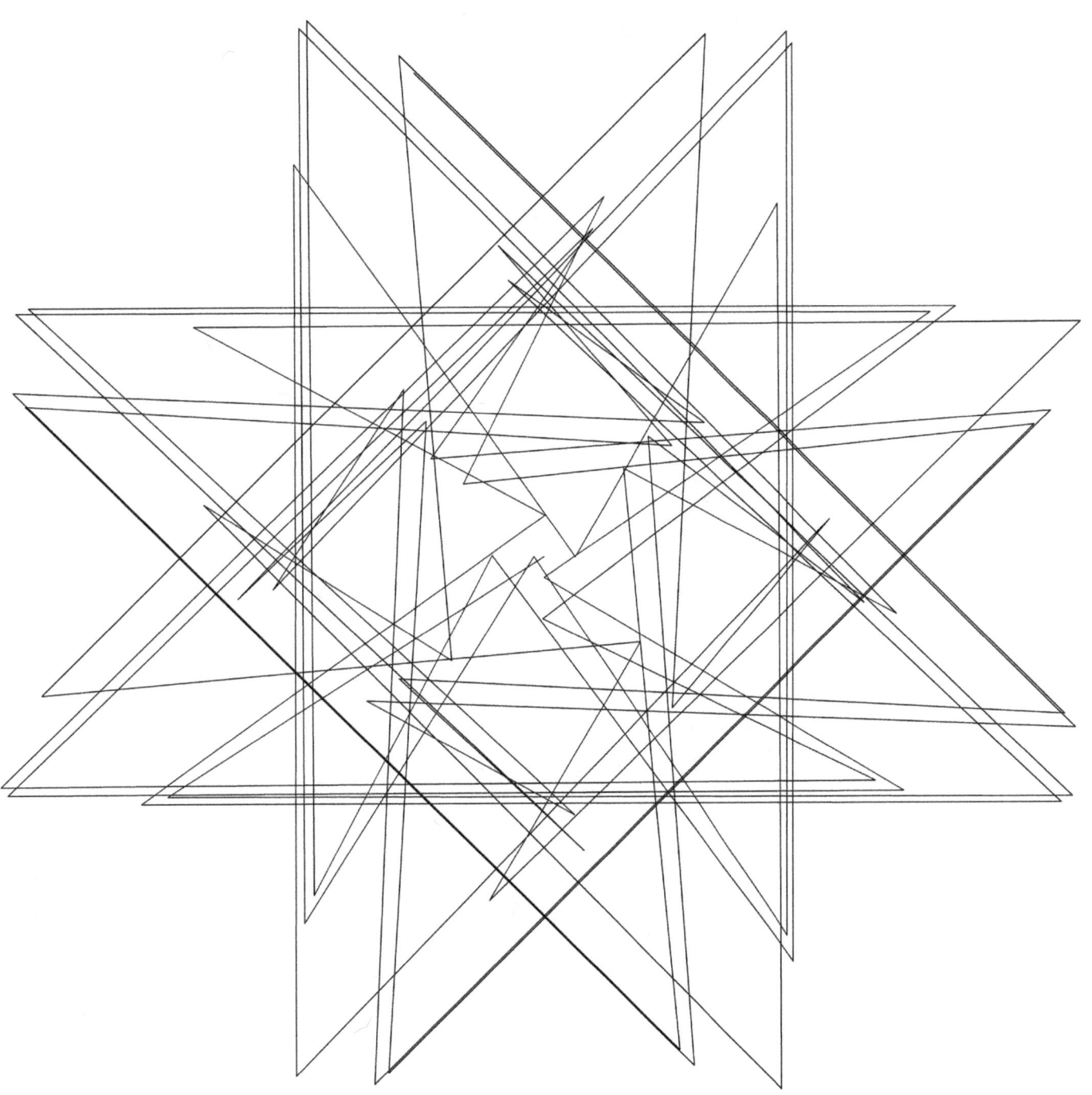

For more of my data adventures and math artwork, kindly visit me at aRtVerse (art-verse.com)!

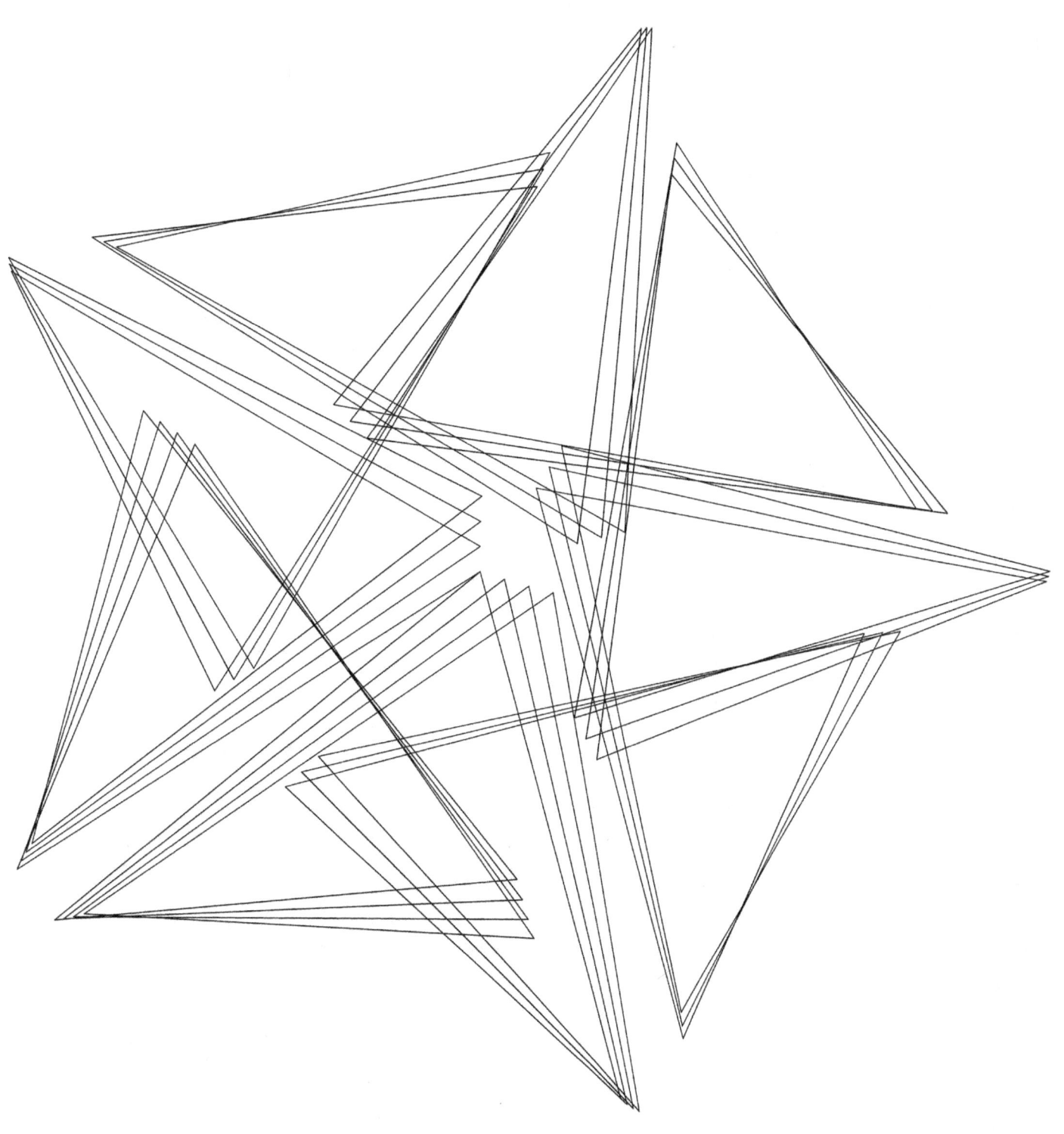

For more of my data adventures and math artwork, kindly visit me at aRtVerse (art-verse.com)!

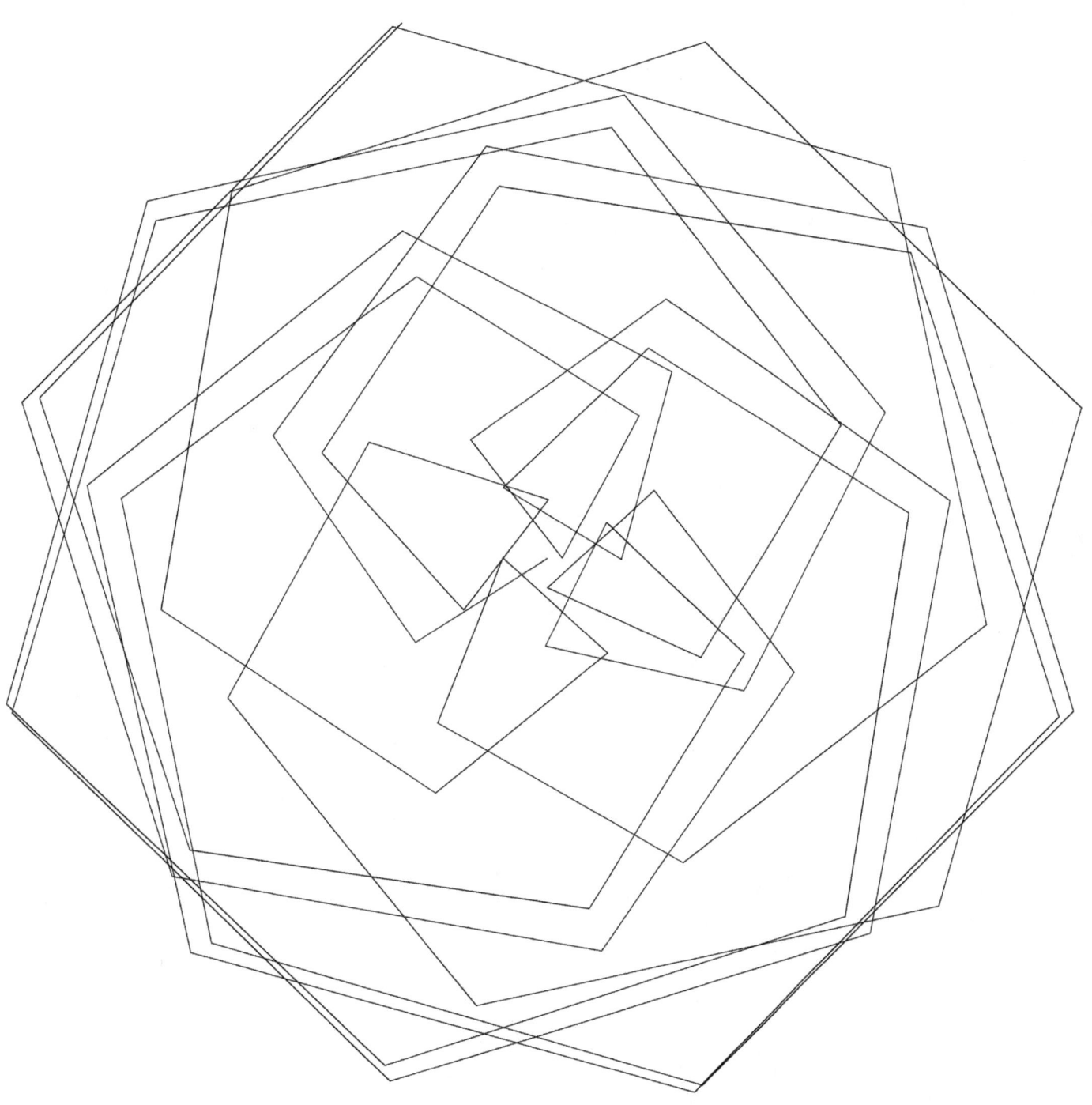

For more of my data adventures and math artwork, kindly visit me at aRtVerse (art-verse.com)!

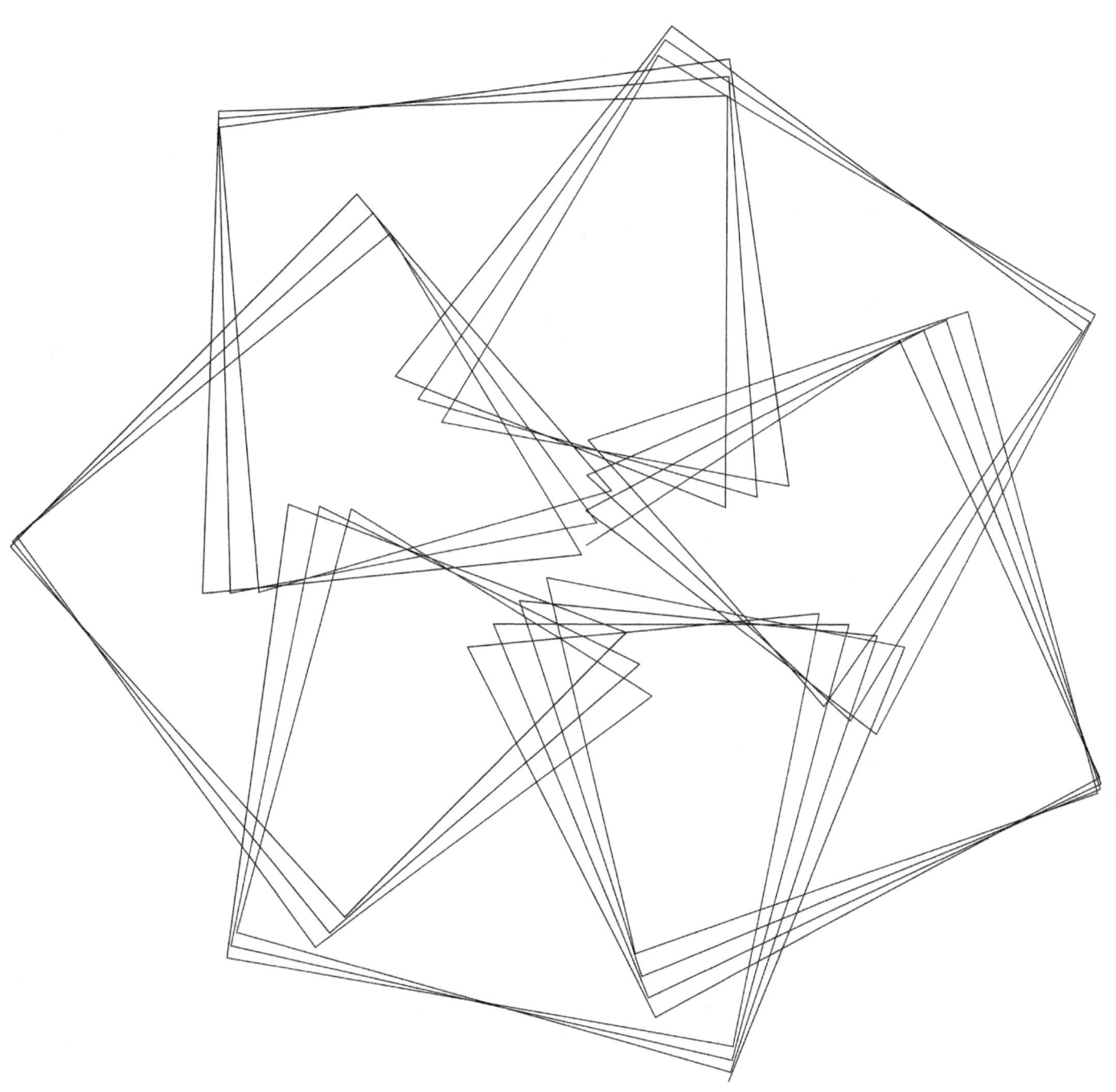

For more of my data adventures and math artwork, kindly visit me at aRtVerse (art-verse.com)!

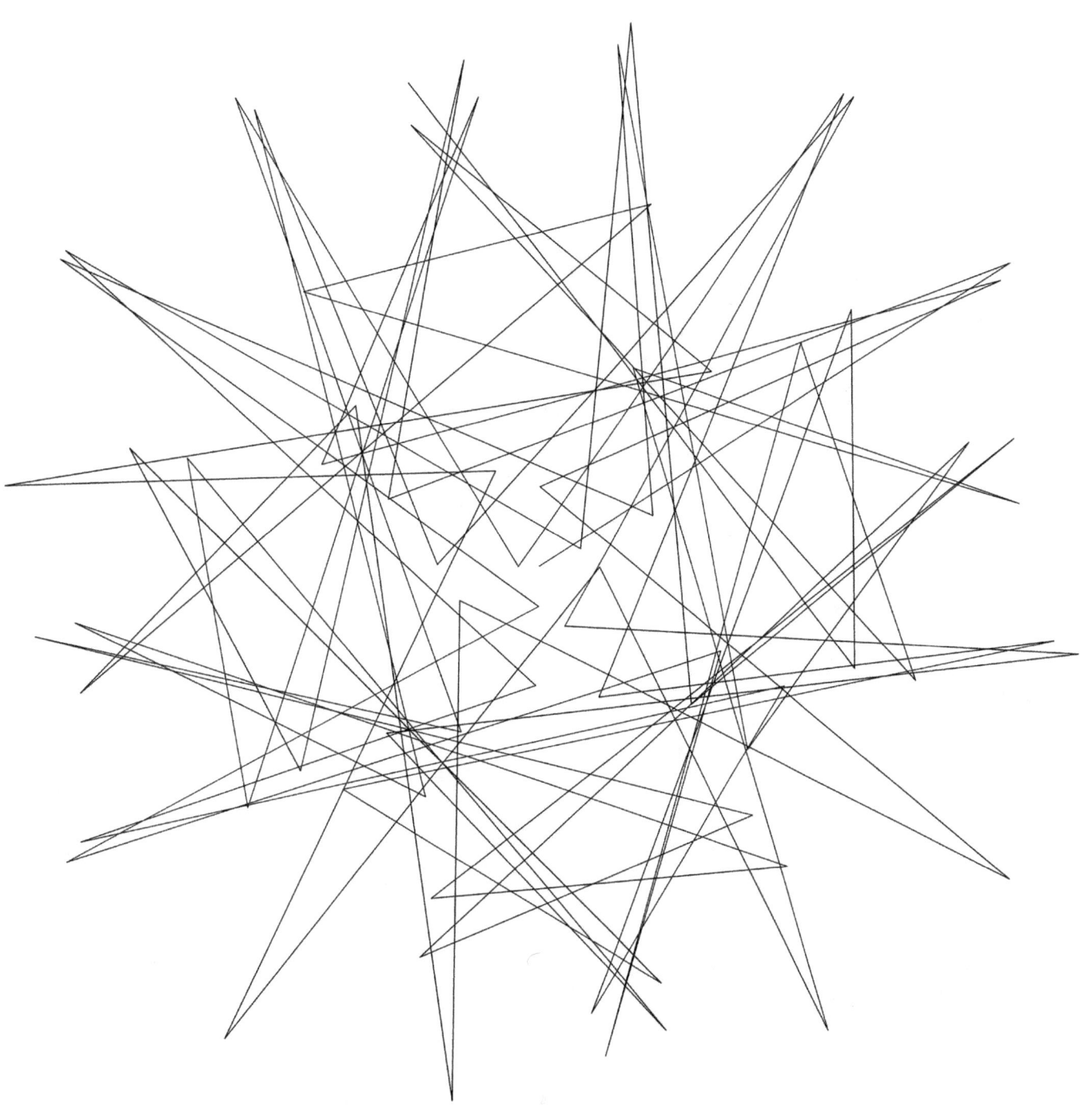

For more of my data adventures and math artwork, kindly visit me at aRtVerse (art-verse.com)!

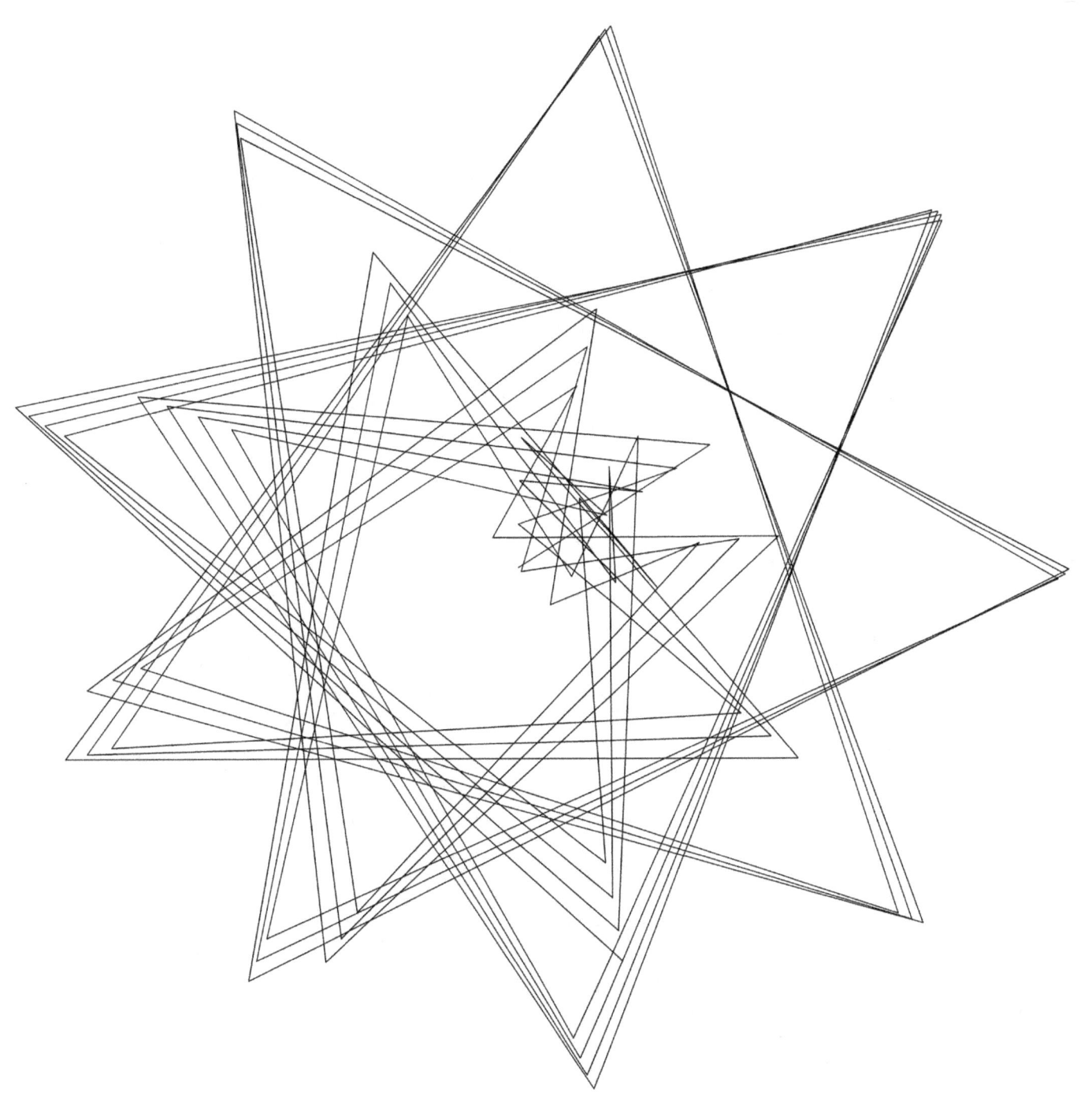

For more of my data adventures and math artwork, kindly visit me at aRtVerse (art-verse.com)!

20

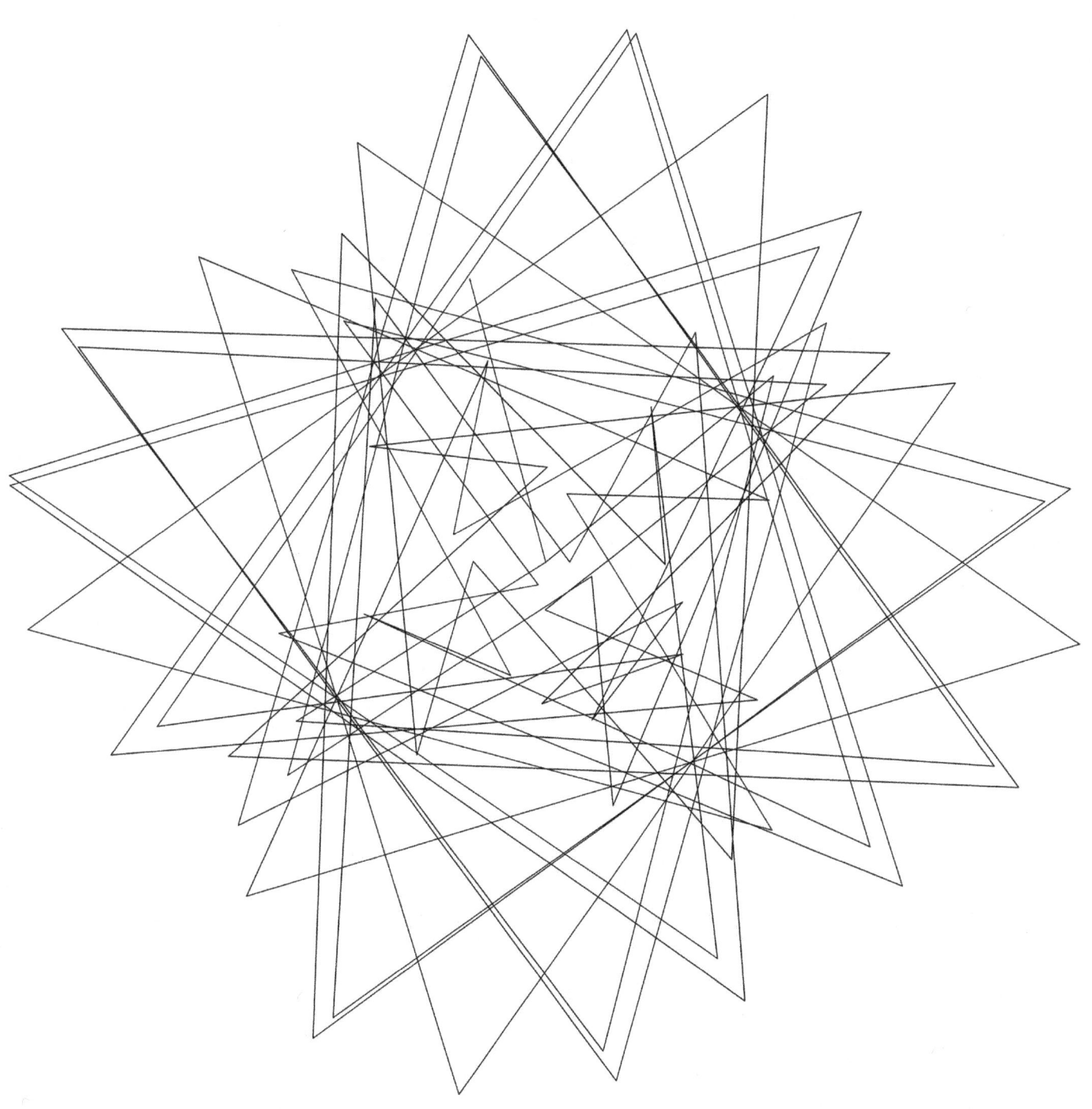

For more of my data adventures and math artwork, kindly visit me at aRtVerse (art-verse.com)!

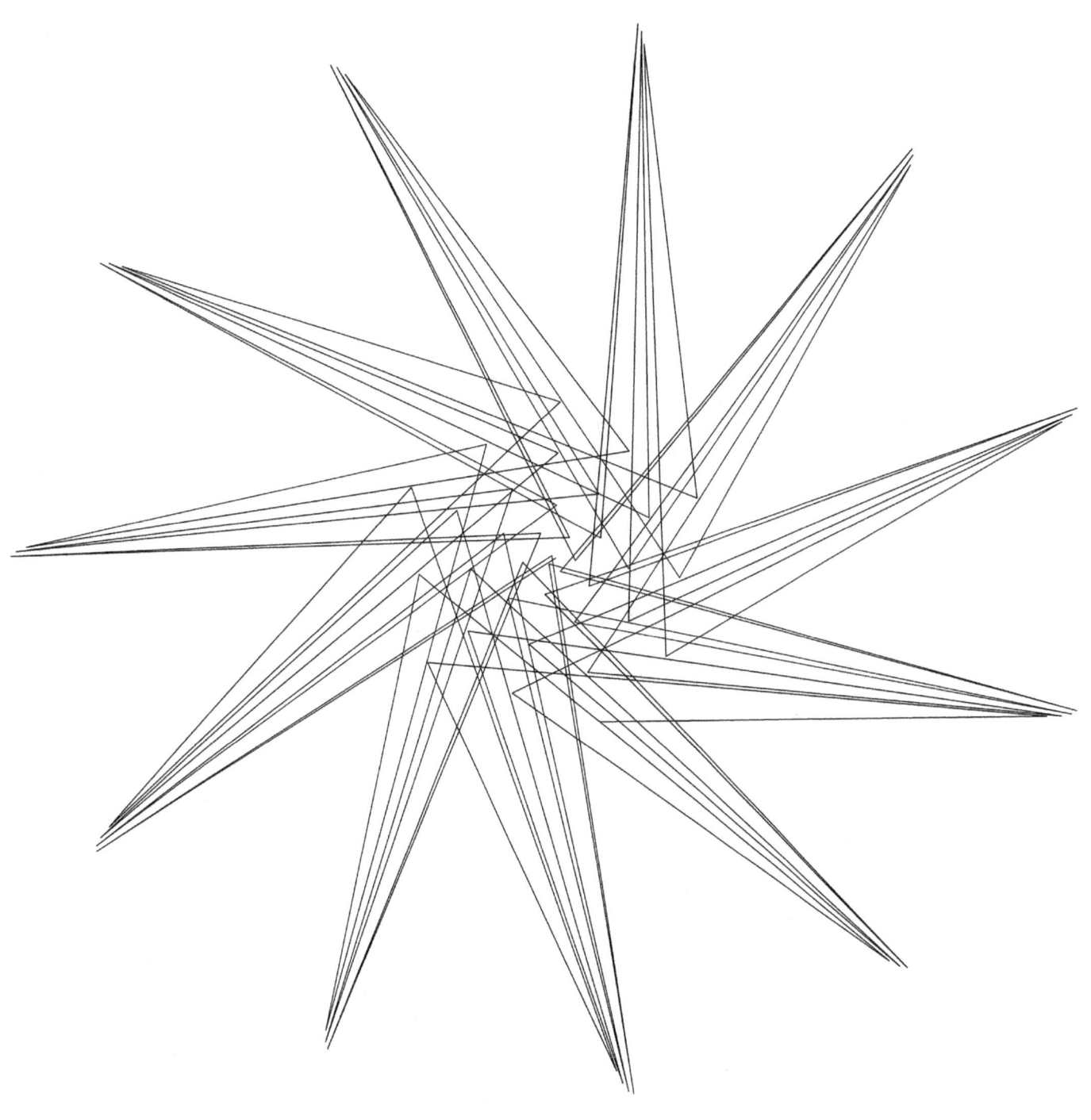

For more of my data adventures and math artwork, kindly visit me at aRtVerse (art-verse.com)!

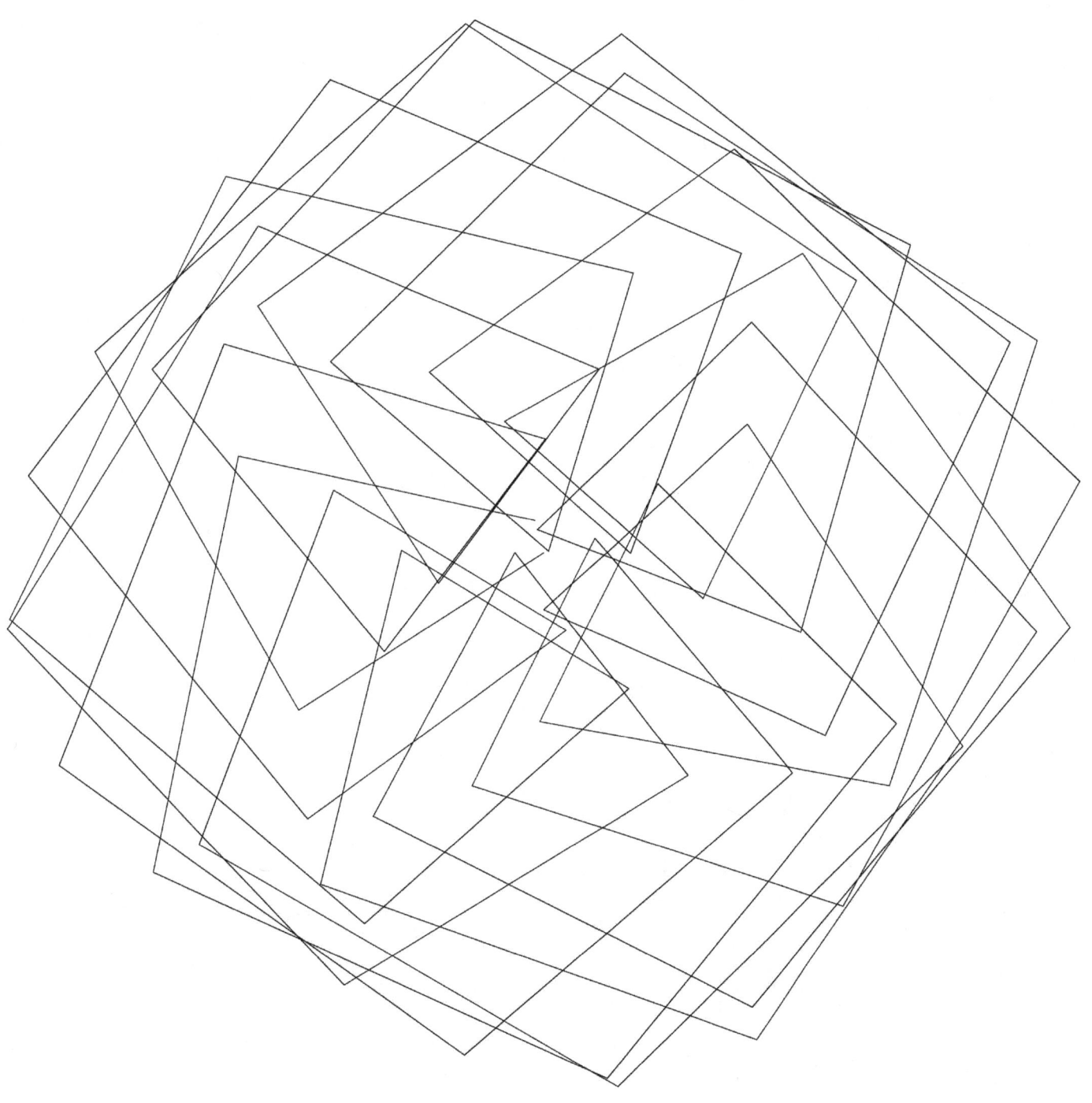

For more of my data adventures and math artwork, kindly visit me at aRtVerse (art-verse.com)!

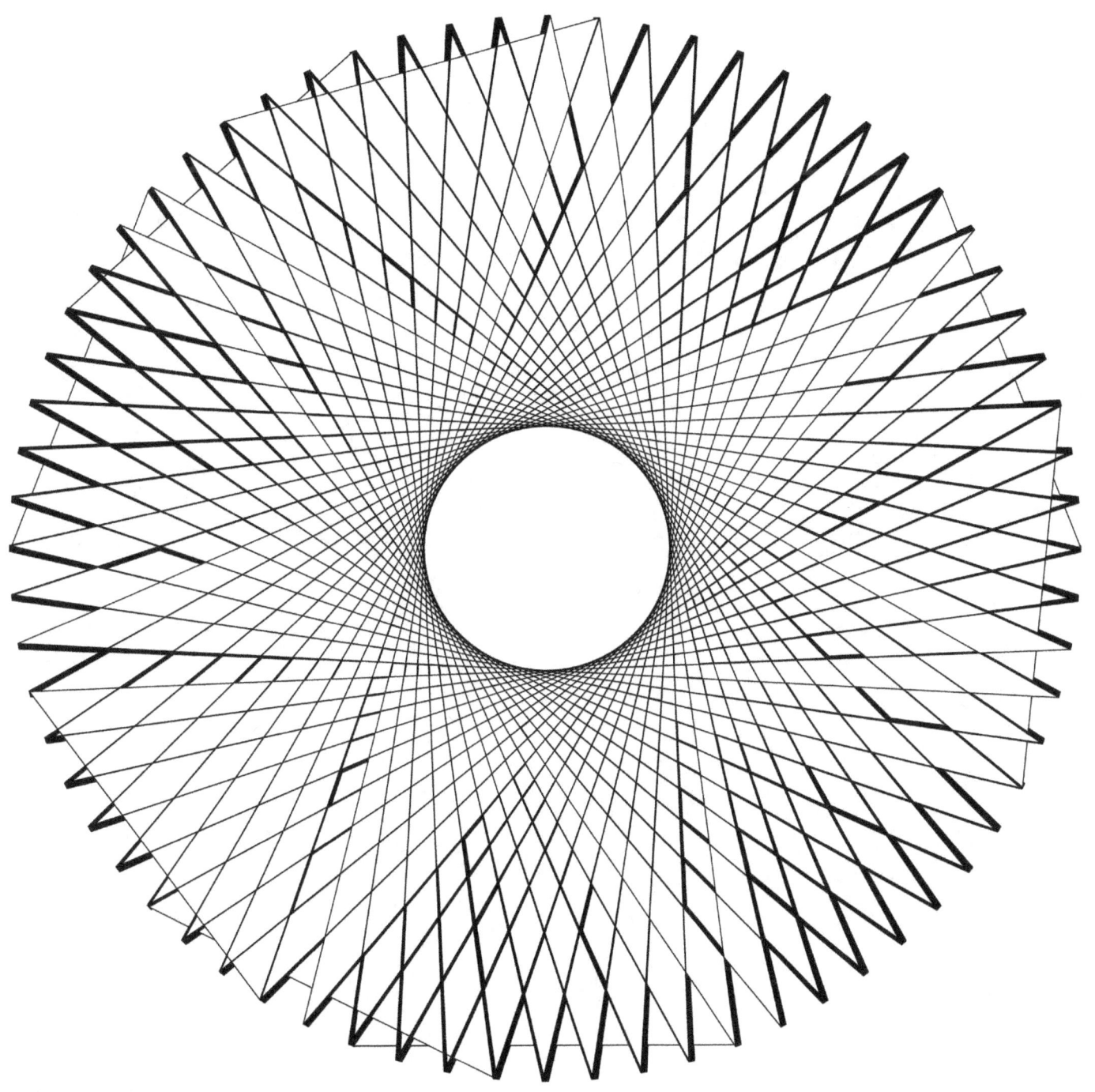

For more of my data adventures and math artwork, kindly visit me at aRtVerse (art-verse.com)!

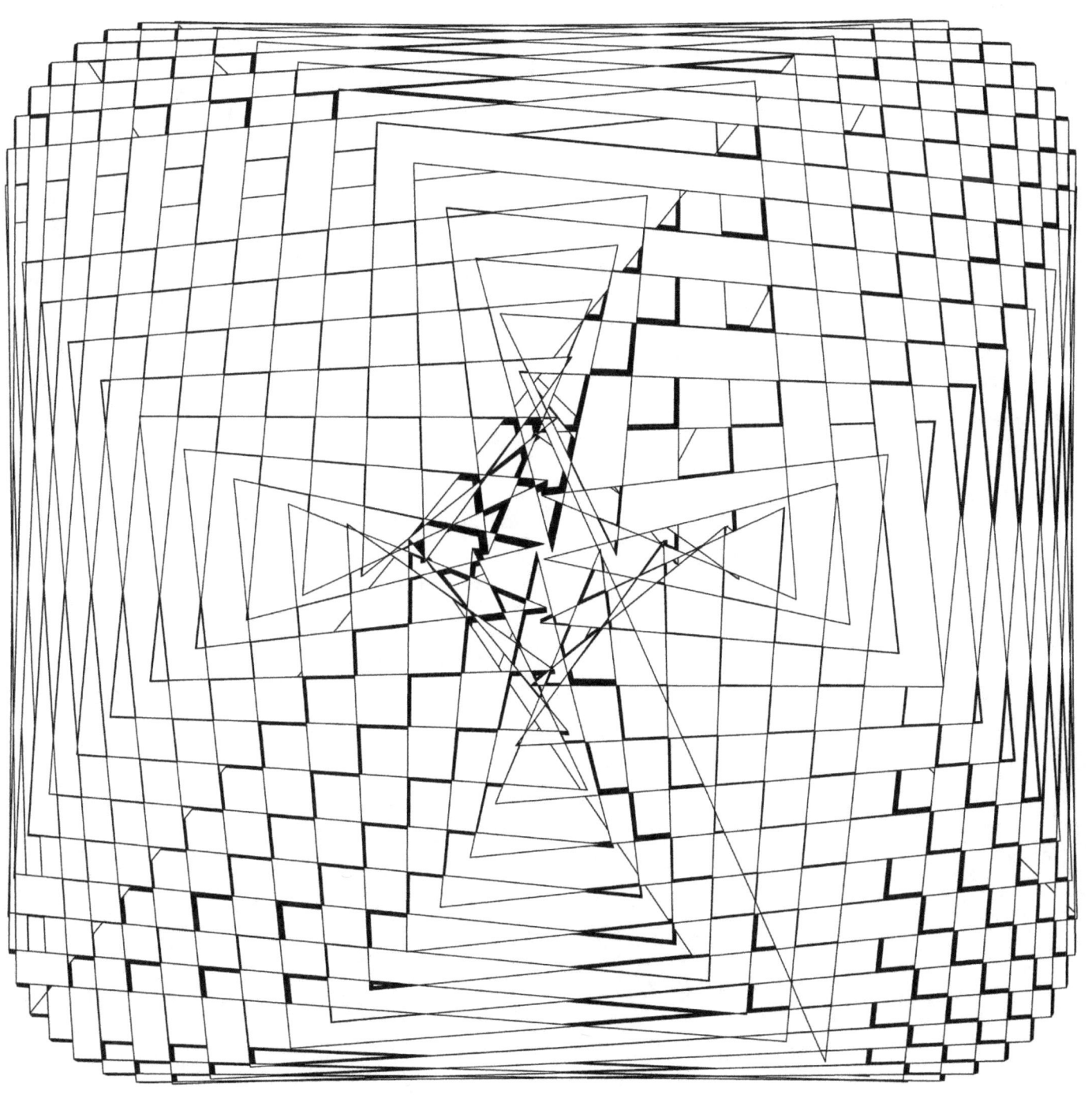

For more of my data adventures and math artwork, kindly visit me at aRtVerse (art-verse.com)!

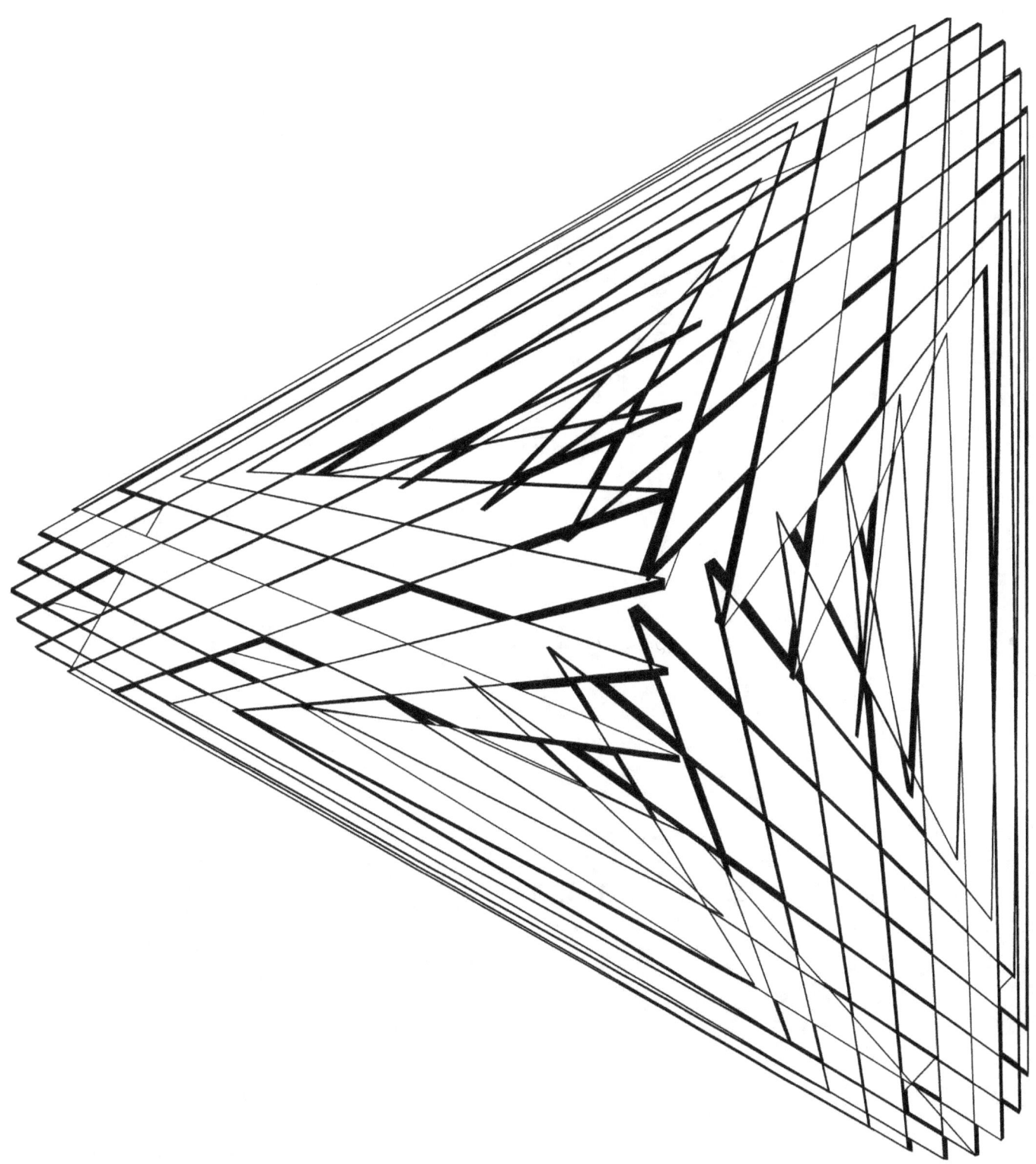

For more of my data adventures and math artwork, kindly visit me at aRtVerse (art-verse.com)!

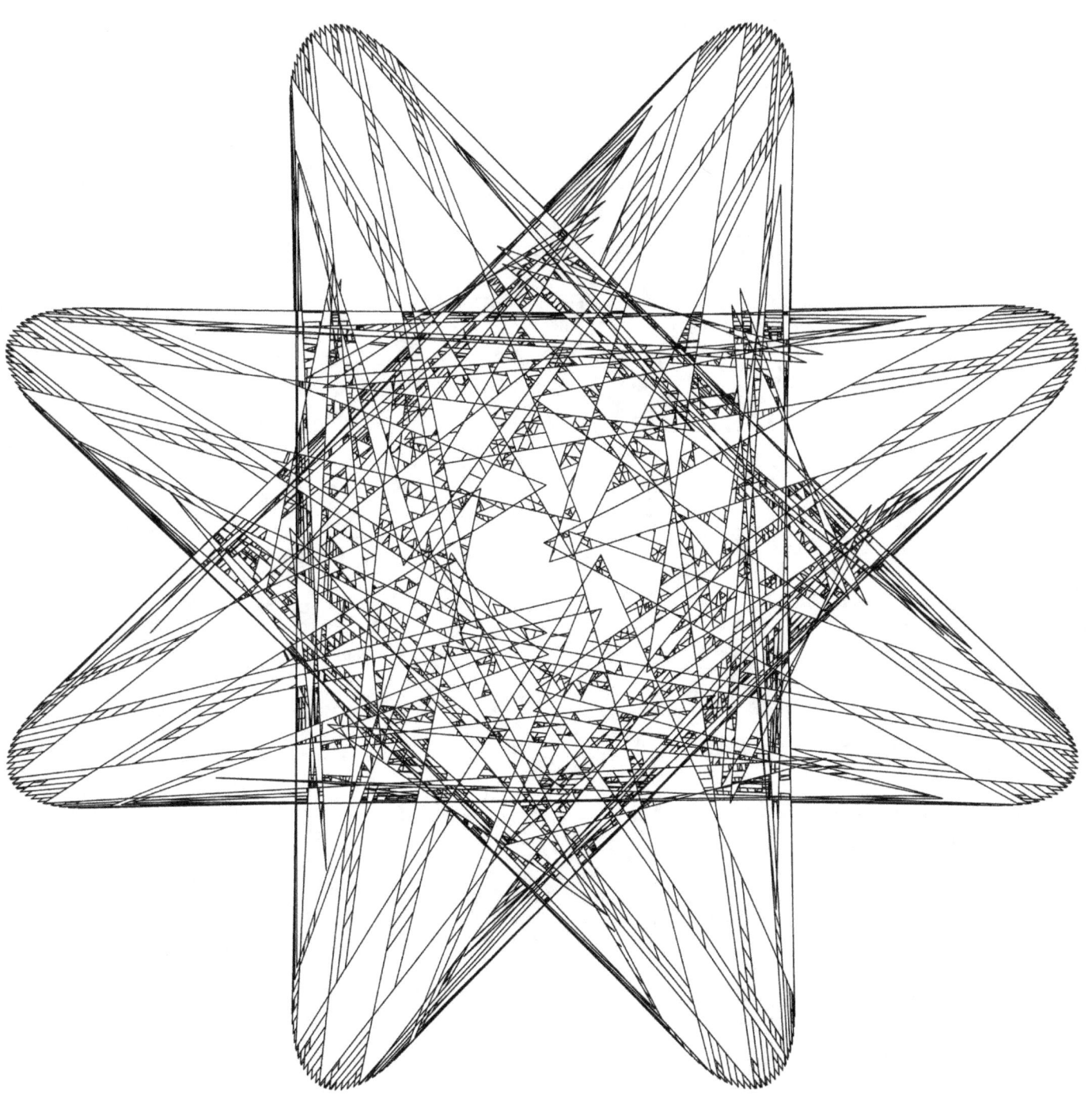

For more of my data adventures and math artwork, kindly visit me at aRtVerse (art-verse.com)!

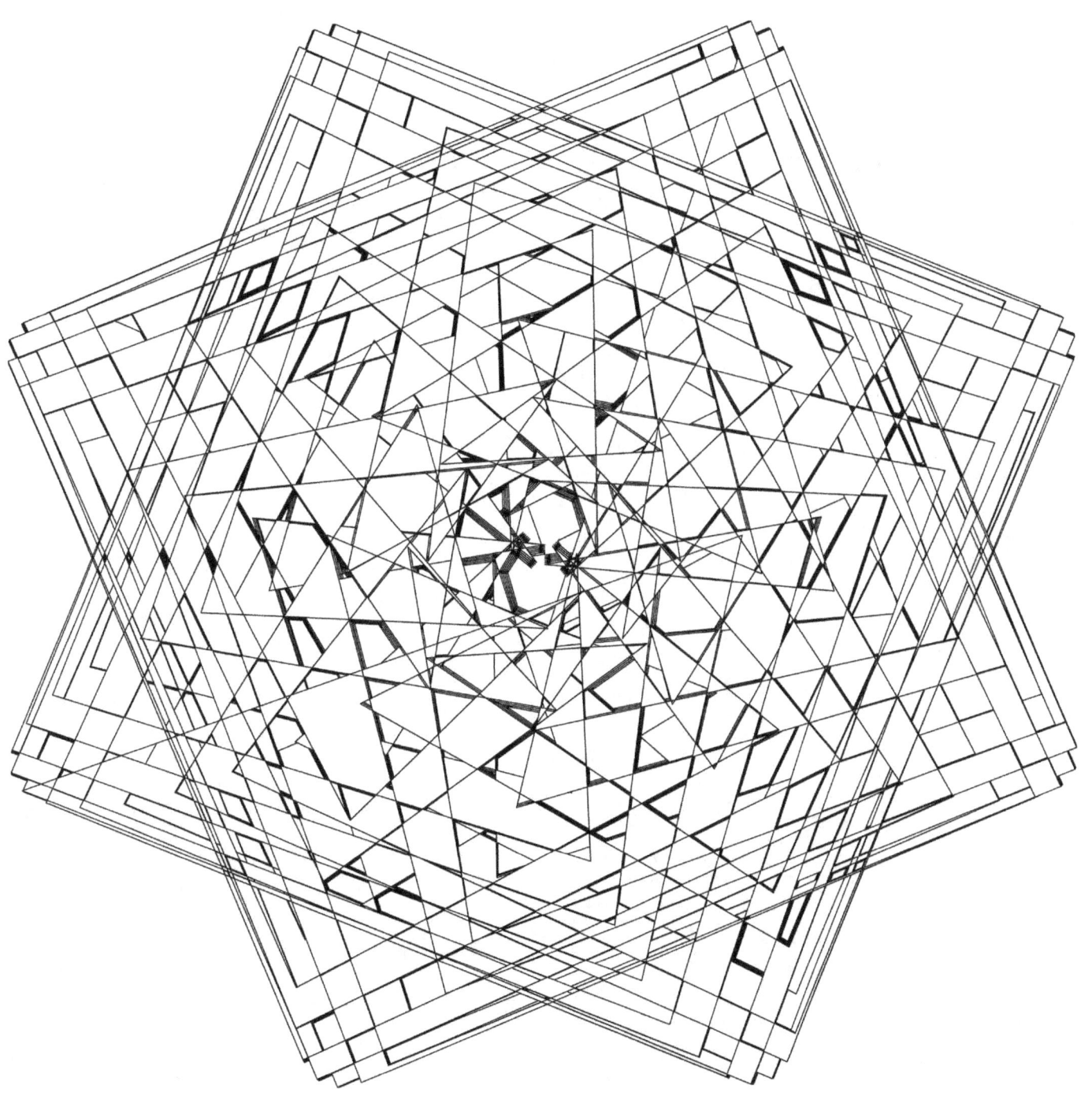

For more of my data adventures and math artwork, kindly visit me at aRtVerse (art-verse.com)!

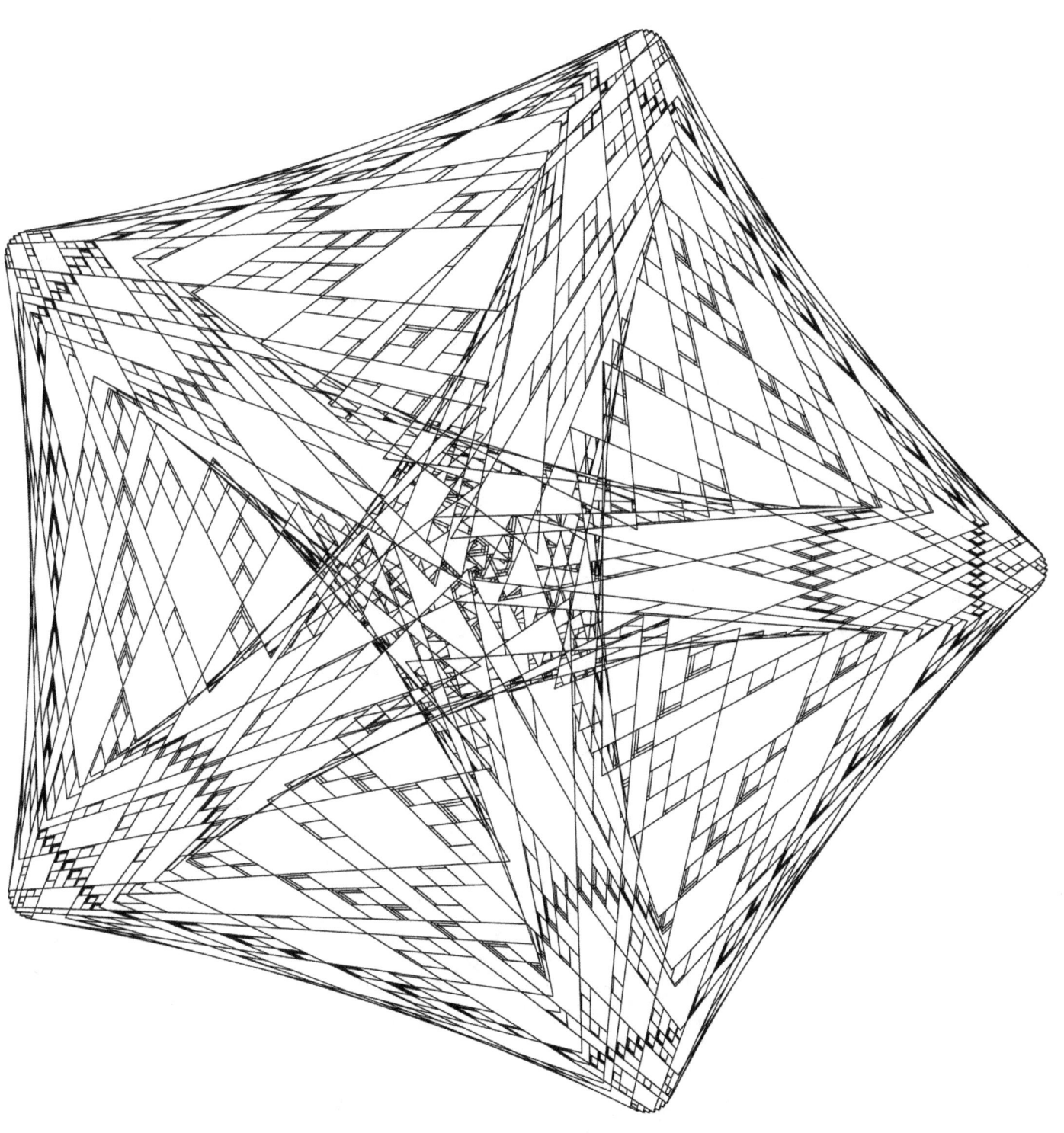

For more of my data adventures and math artwork, kindly visit me at aRtVerse (art-verse.com)!

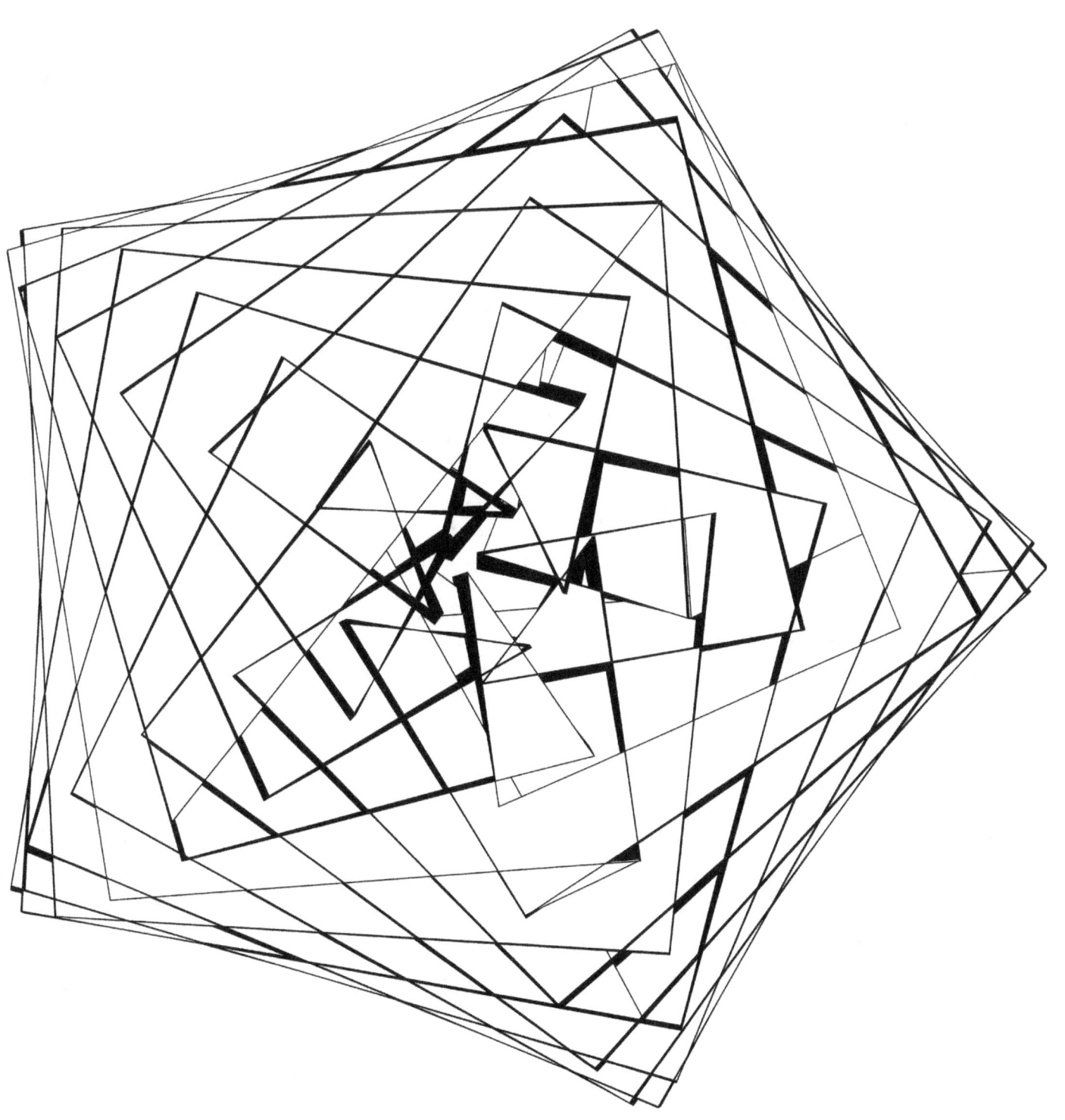

For more of my data adventures and math artwork, kindly visit me at aRtVerse (art-verse.com)!

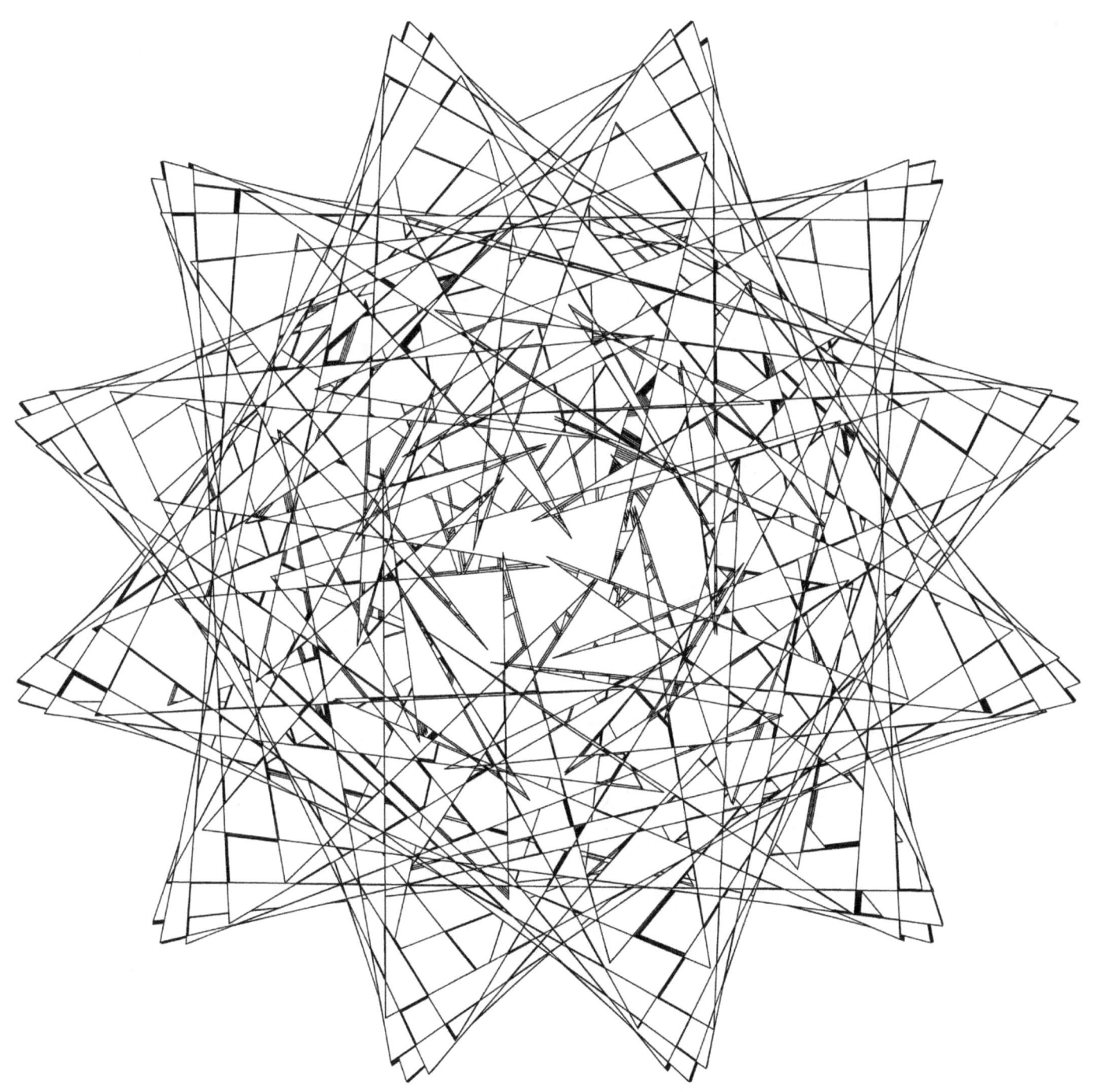

For more of my data adventures and math artwork, kindly visit me at aRtVerse (art-verse.com)!

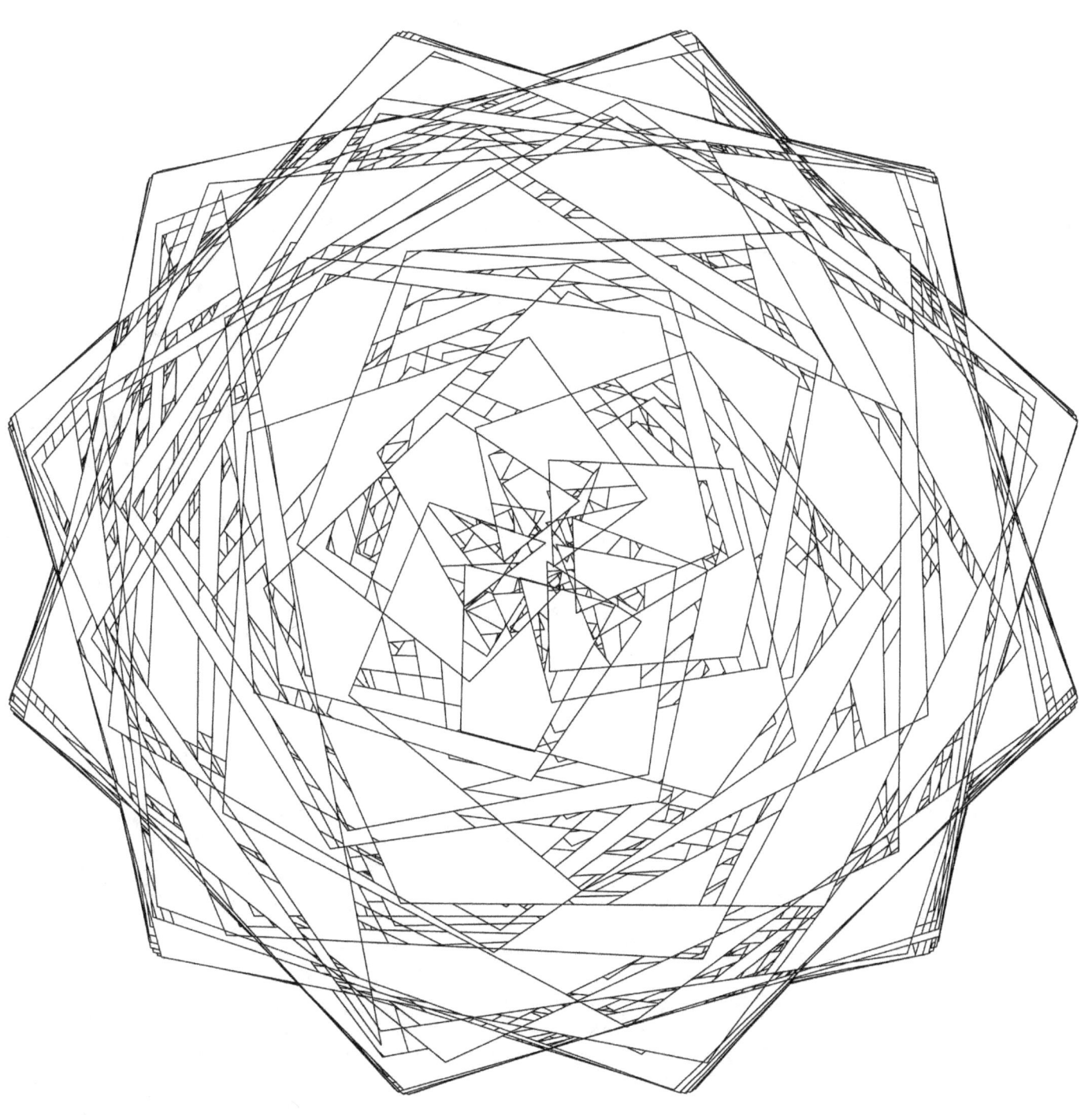

For more of my data adventures and math artwork, kindly visit me at aRtVerse (art-verse.com)!

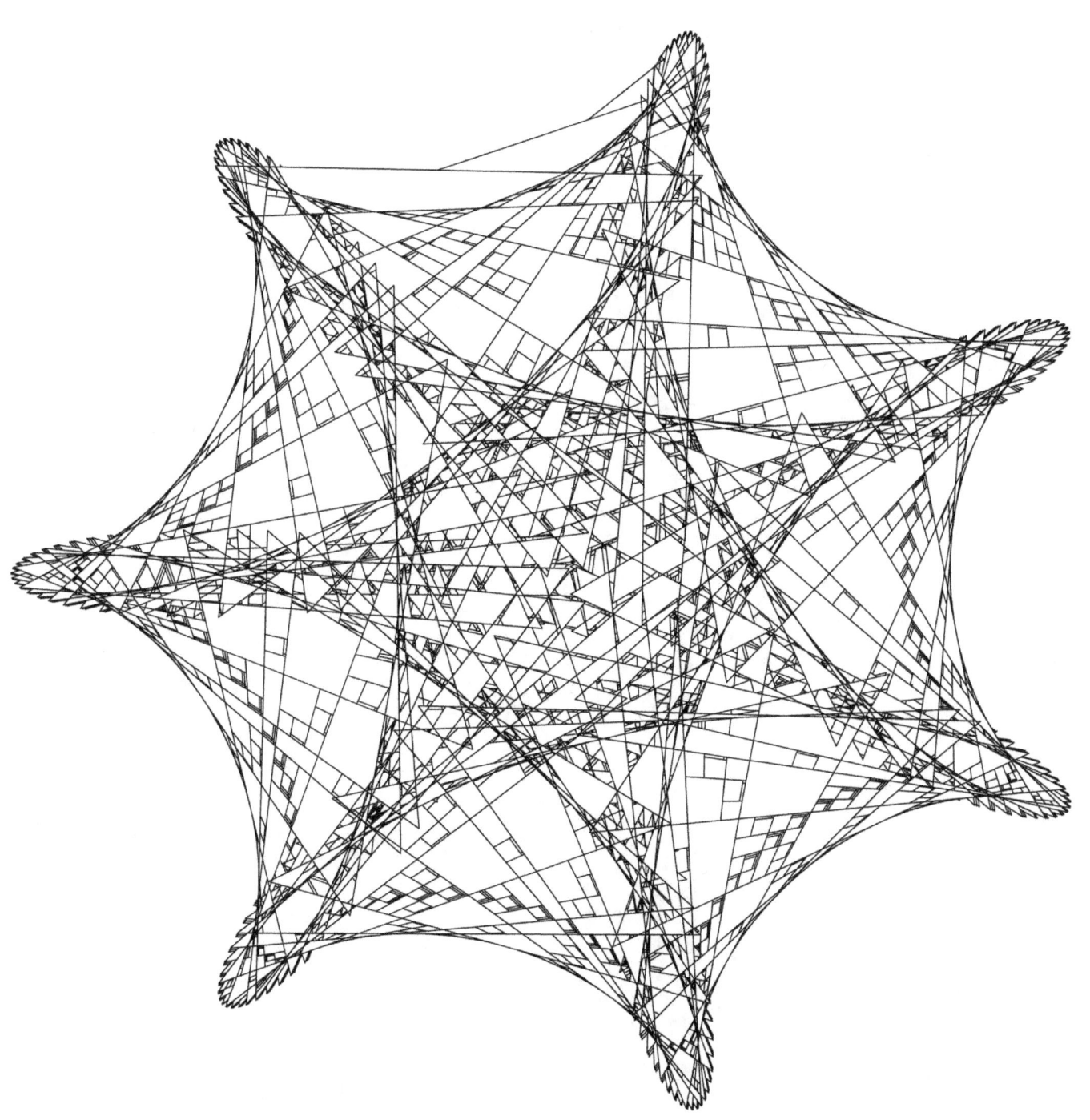

For more of my data adventures and math artwork, kindly visit me at aRtVerse (art-verse.com)!

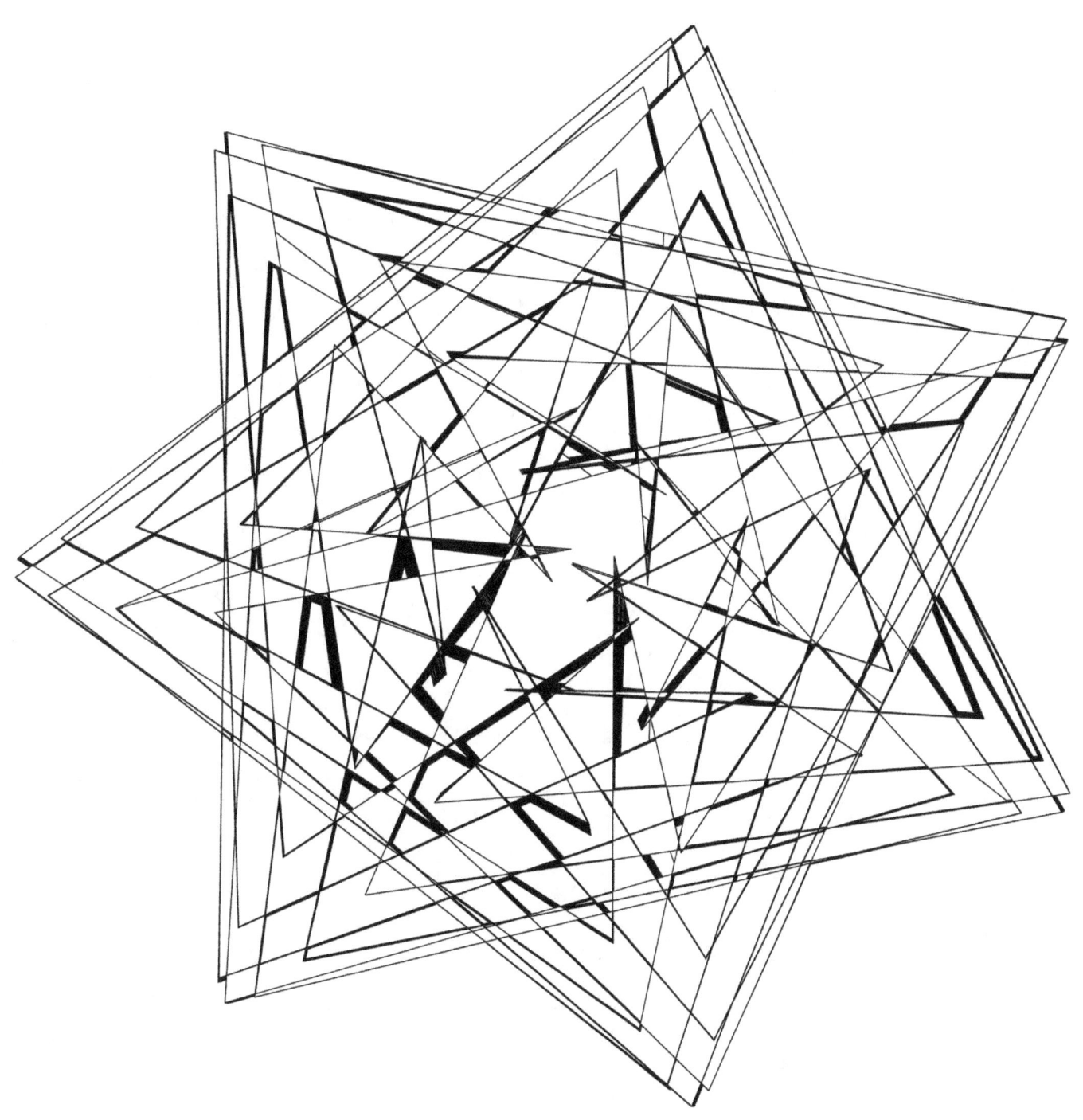

For more of my data adventures and math artwork, kindly visit me at aRtVerse (art-verse.com)!

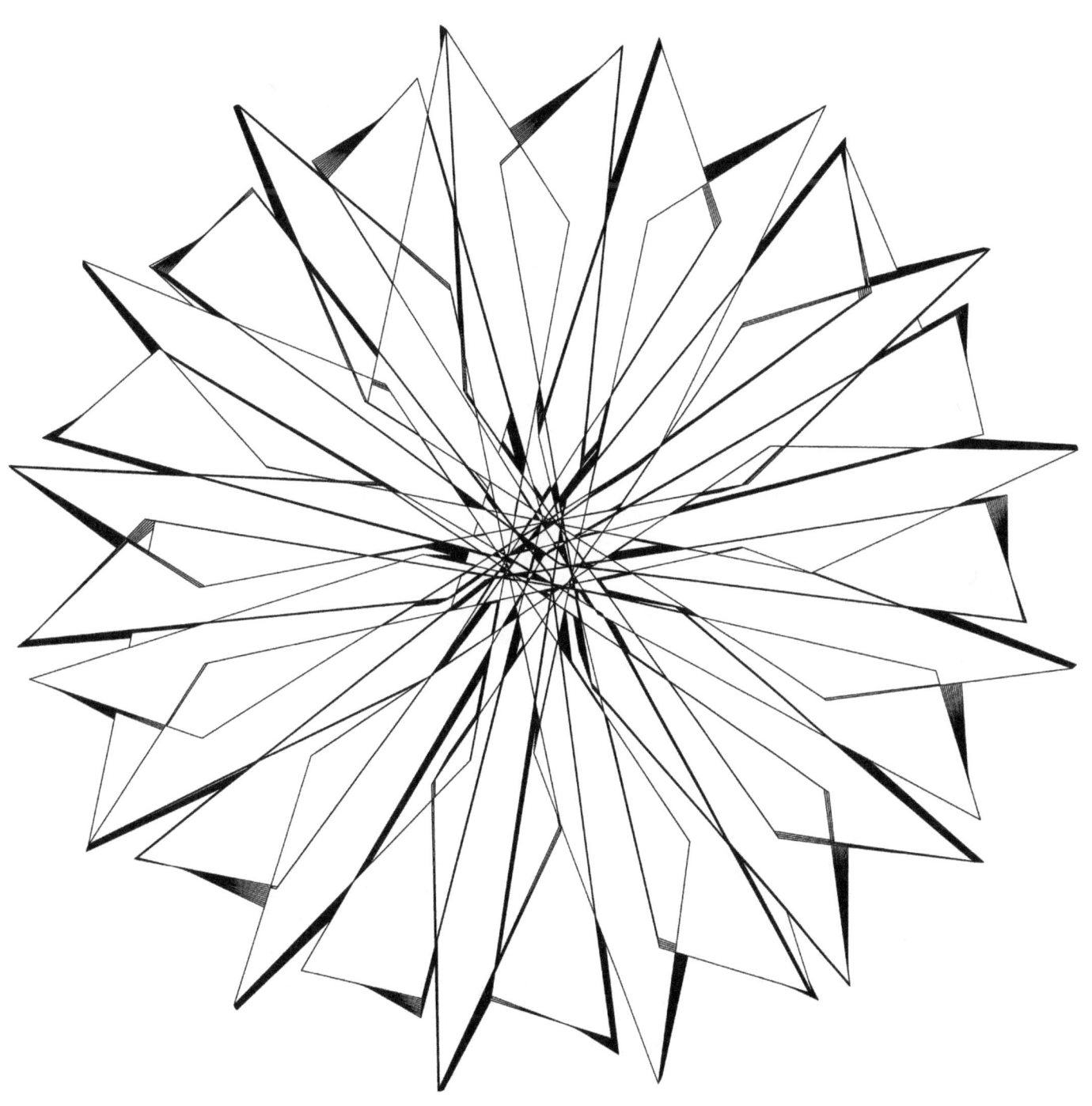

For more of my data adventures and math artwork, kindly visit me at aRtVerse (art-verse.com)!

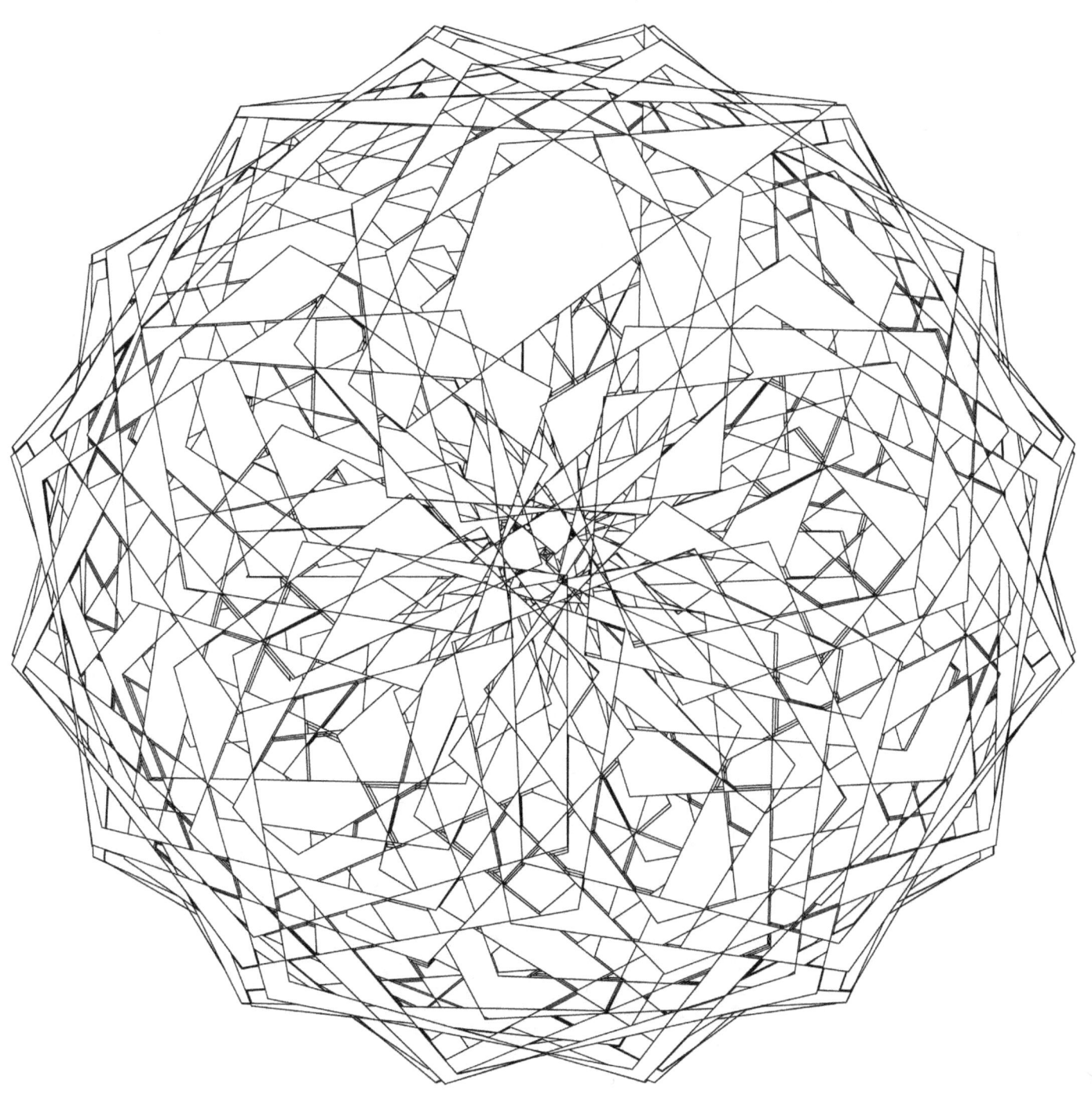

For more of my data adventures and math artwork, kindly visit me at aRtVerse (art-verse.com)!

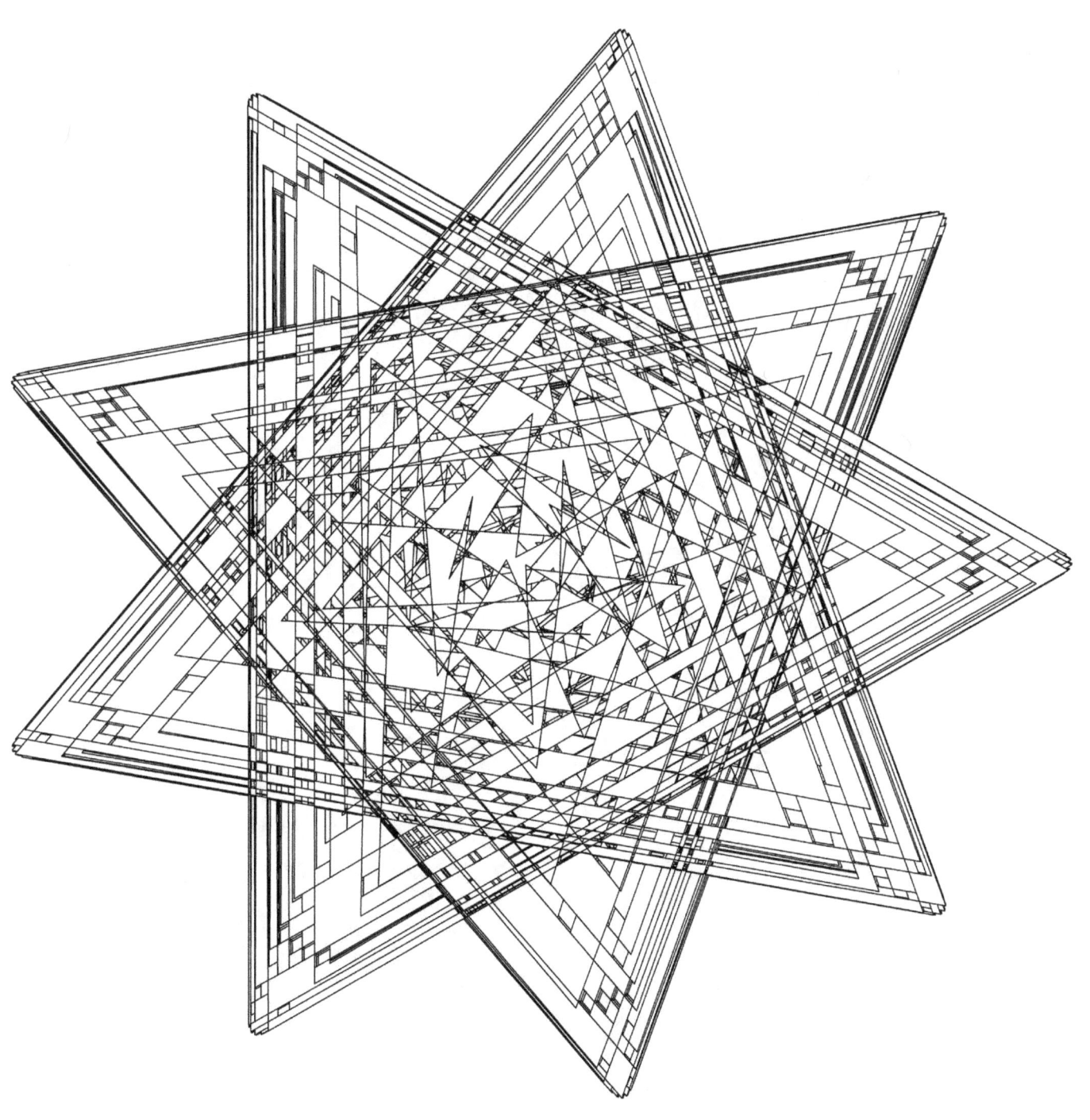

For more of my data adventures and math artwork, kindly visit me at aRtVerse (art-verse.com)!

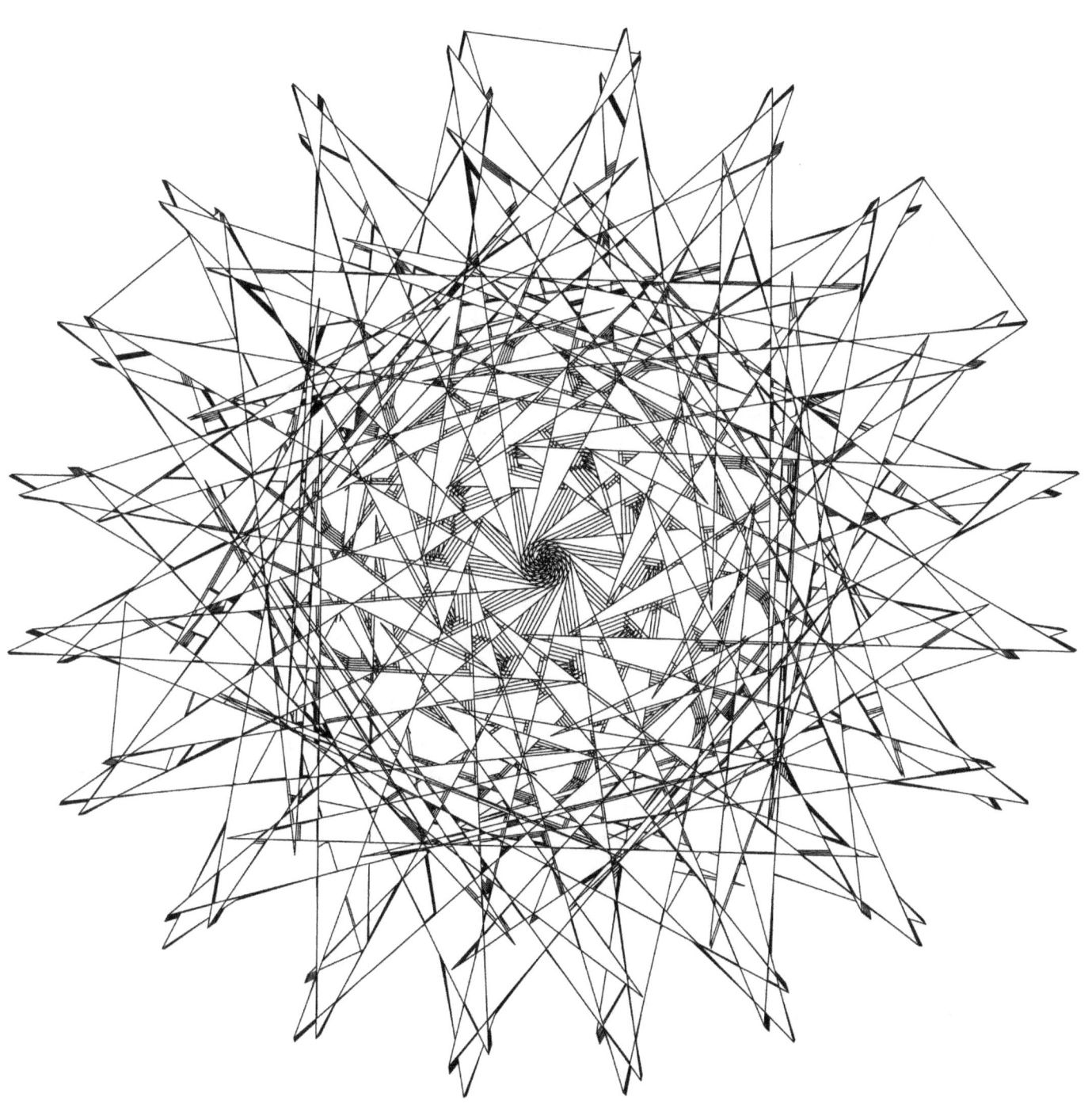

For more of my data adventures and math artwork, kindly visit me at aRtVerse (art-verse.com)!

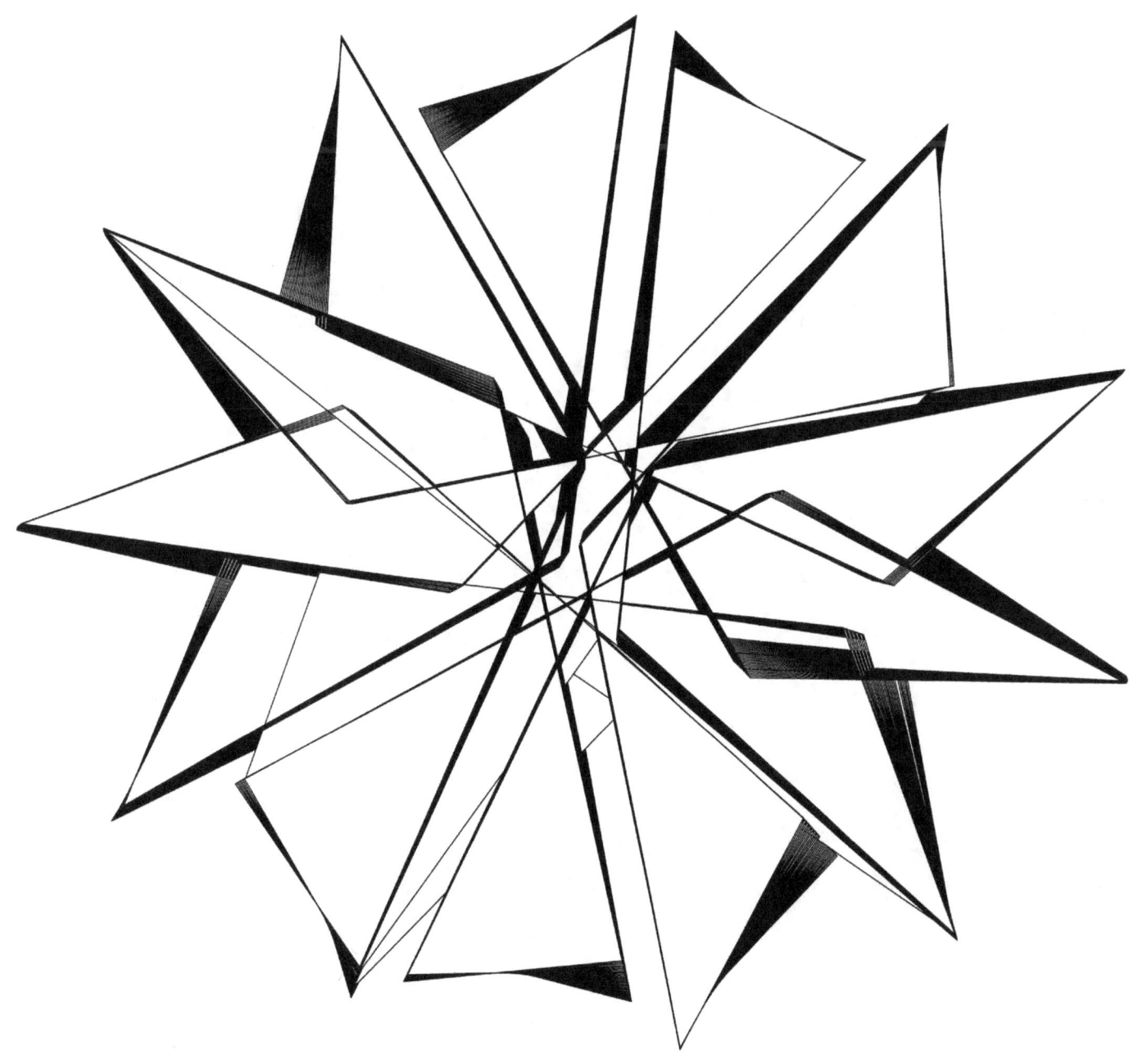

For more of my data adventures and math artwork, kindly visit me at aRtVerse (art-verse.com)!

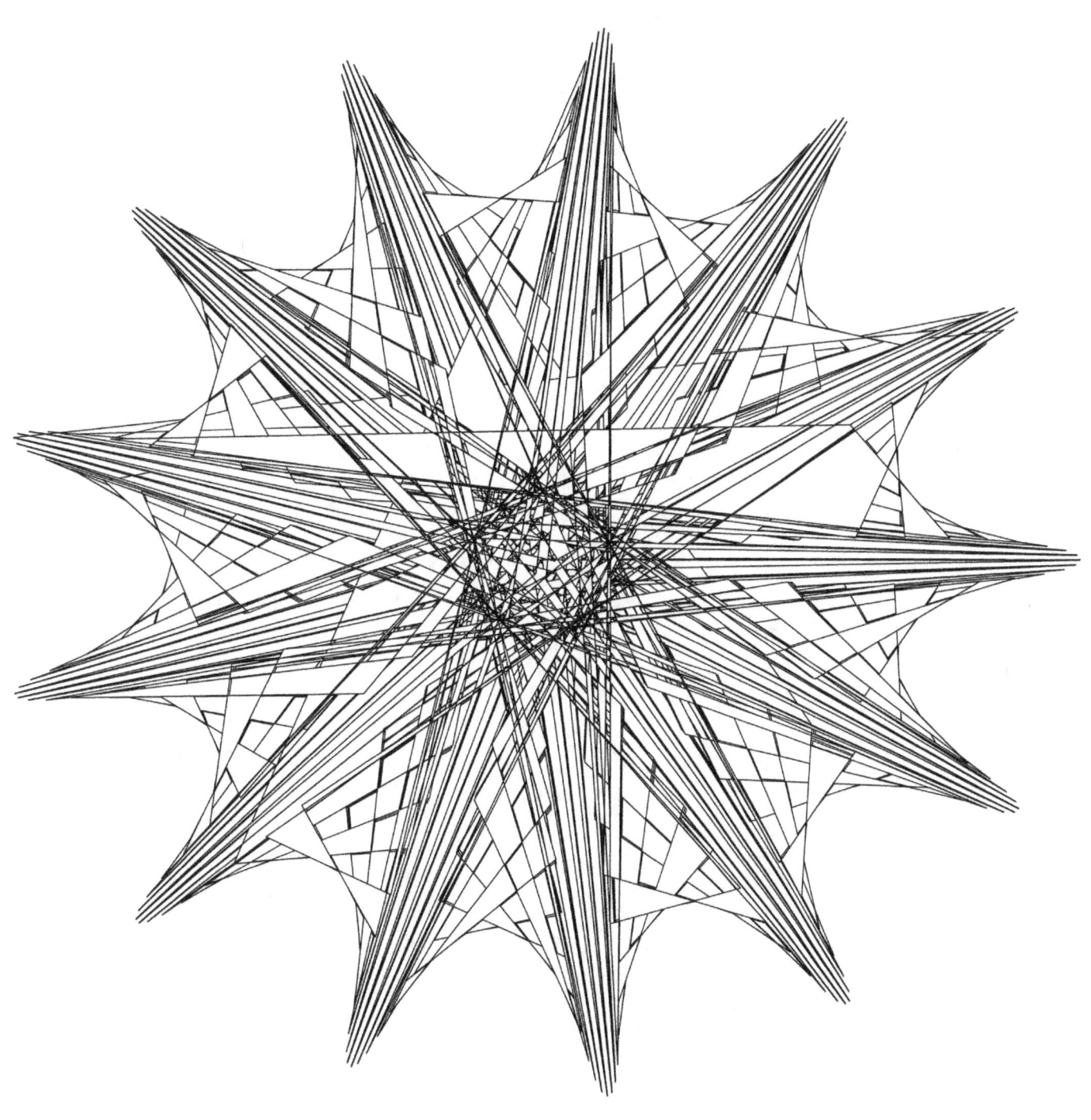

For more of my data adventures and math artwork, kindly visit me at aRtVerse (art-verse.com)!

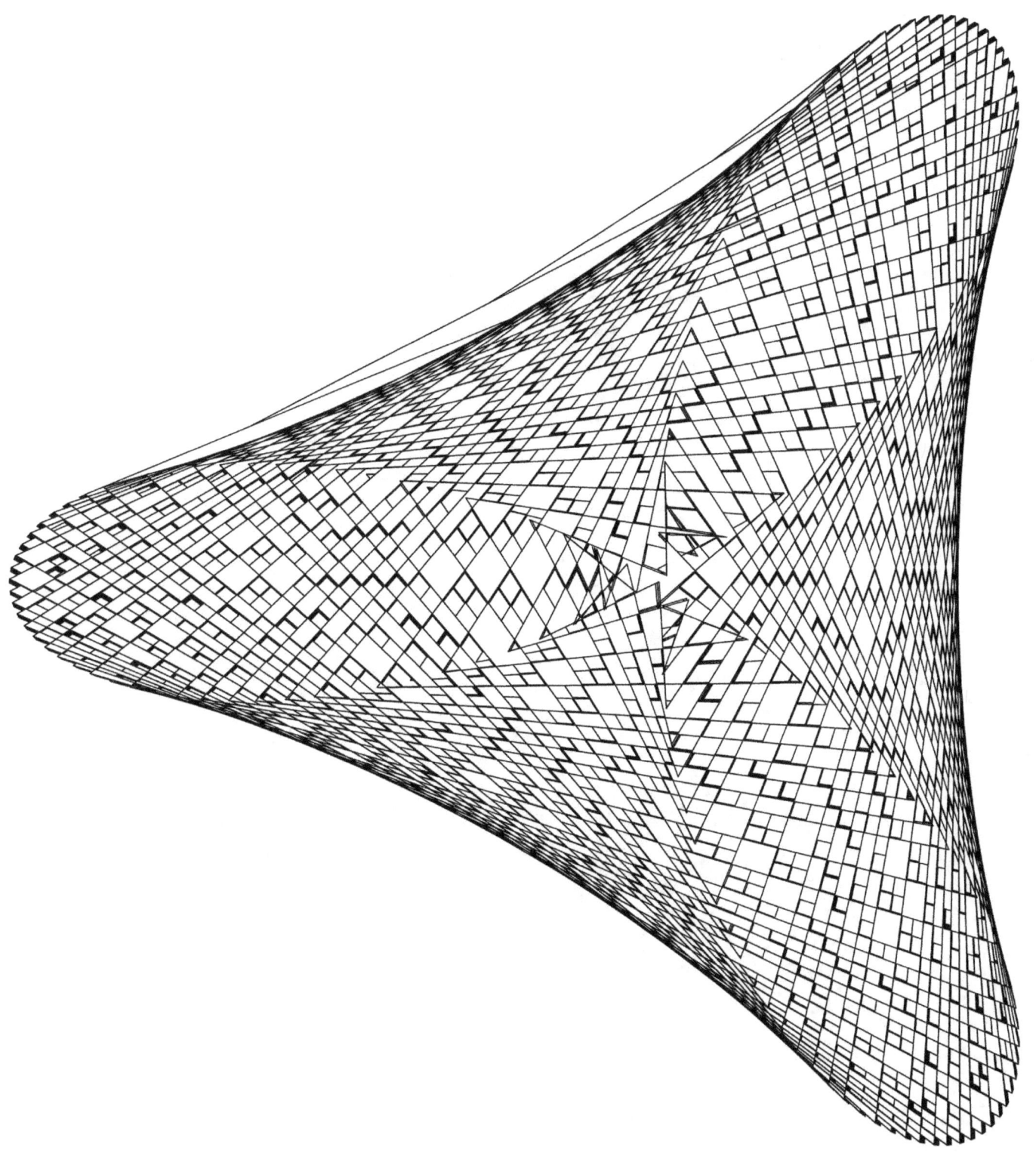

For more of my data adventures and math artwork, kindly visit me at aRtVerse (art-verse.com)!

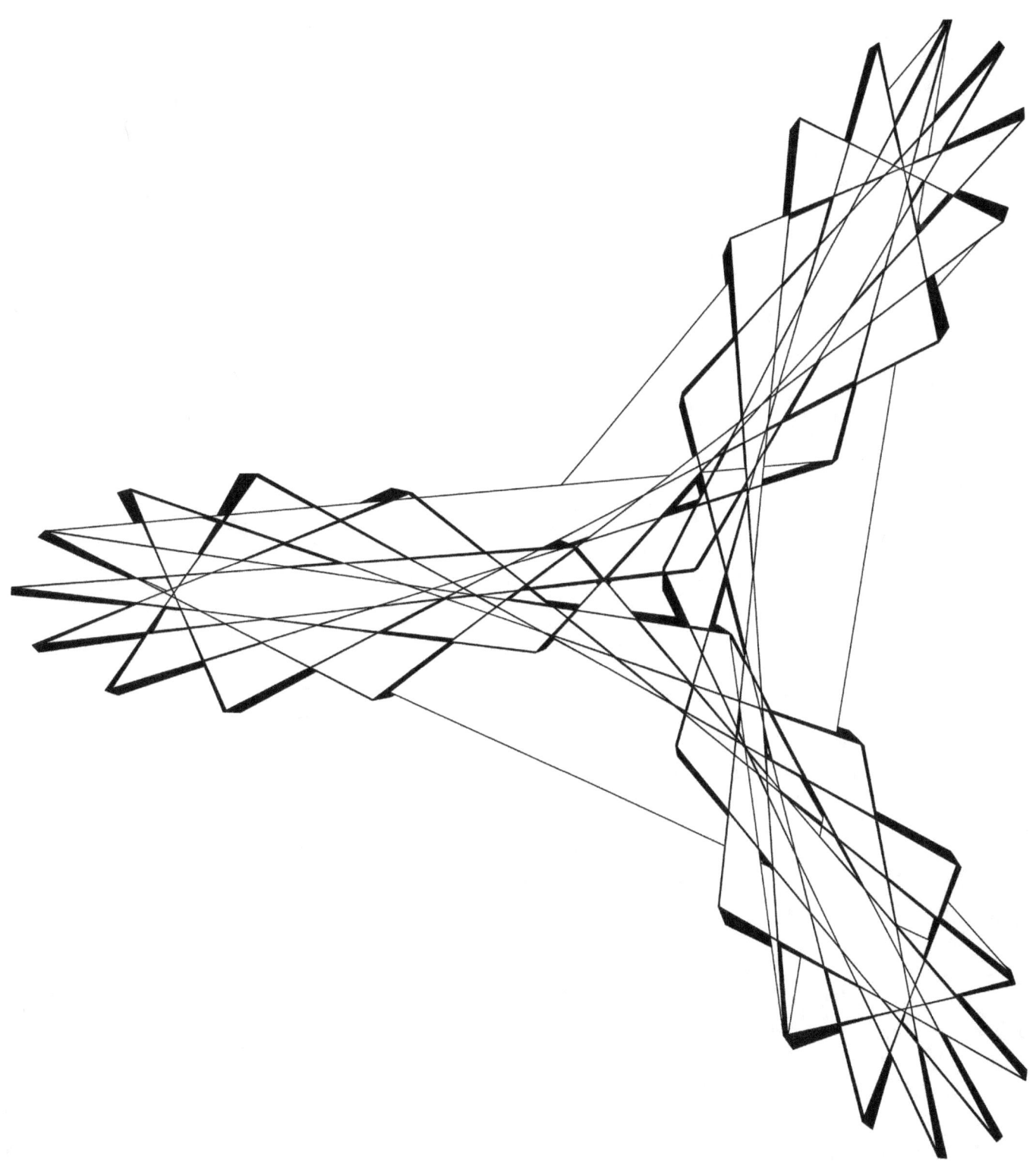

For more of my data adventures and math artwork, kindly visit me at aRtVerse (art-verse.com)!

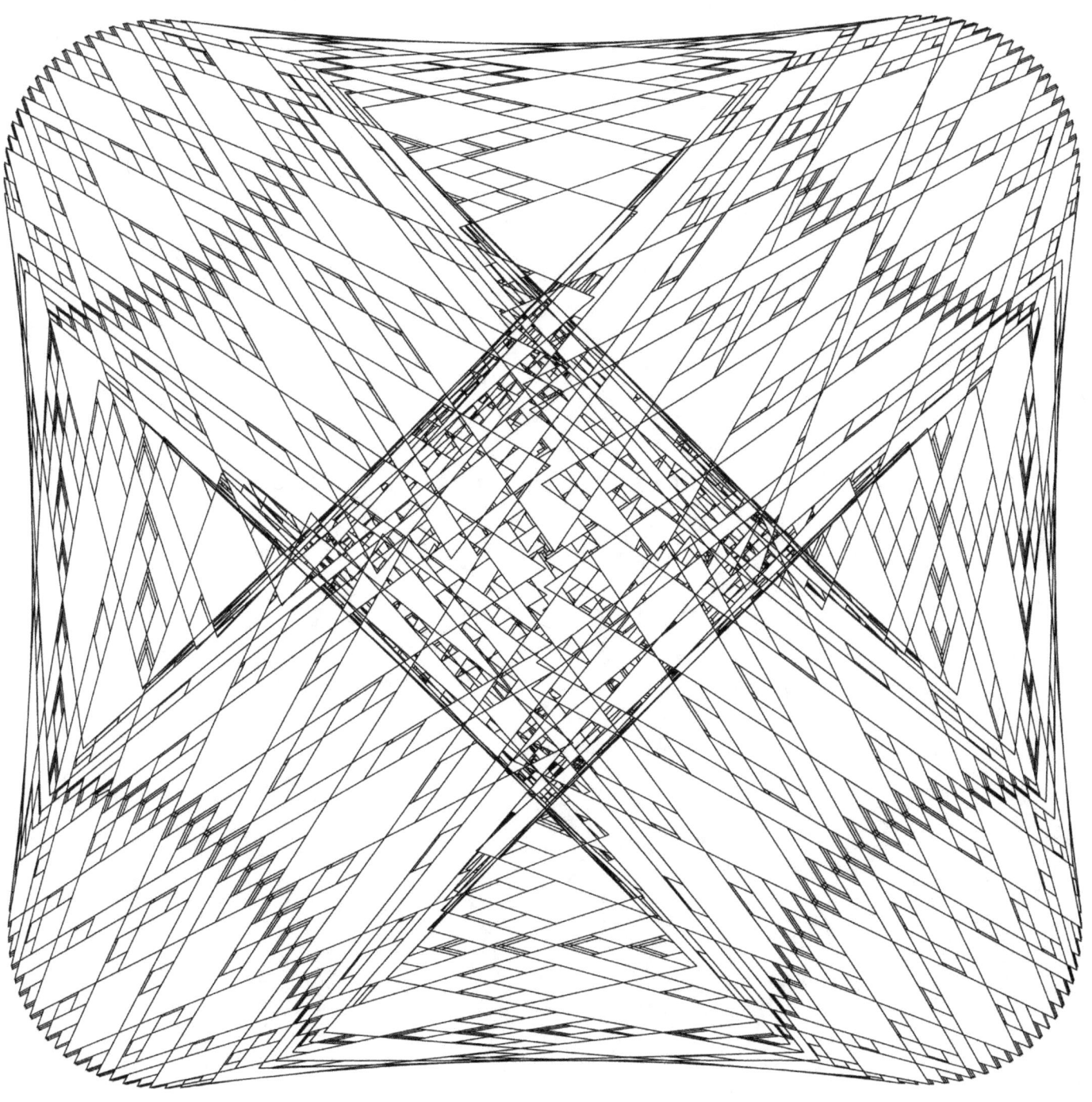

For more of my data adventures and math artwork, kindly visit me at aRtVerse (art-verse.com)!

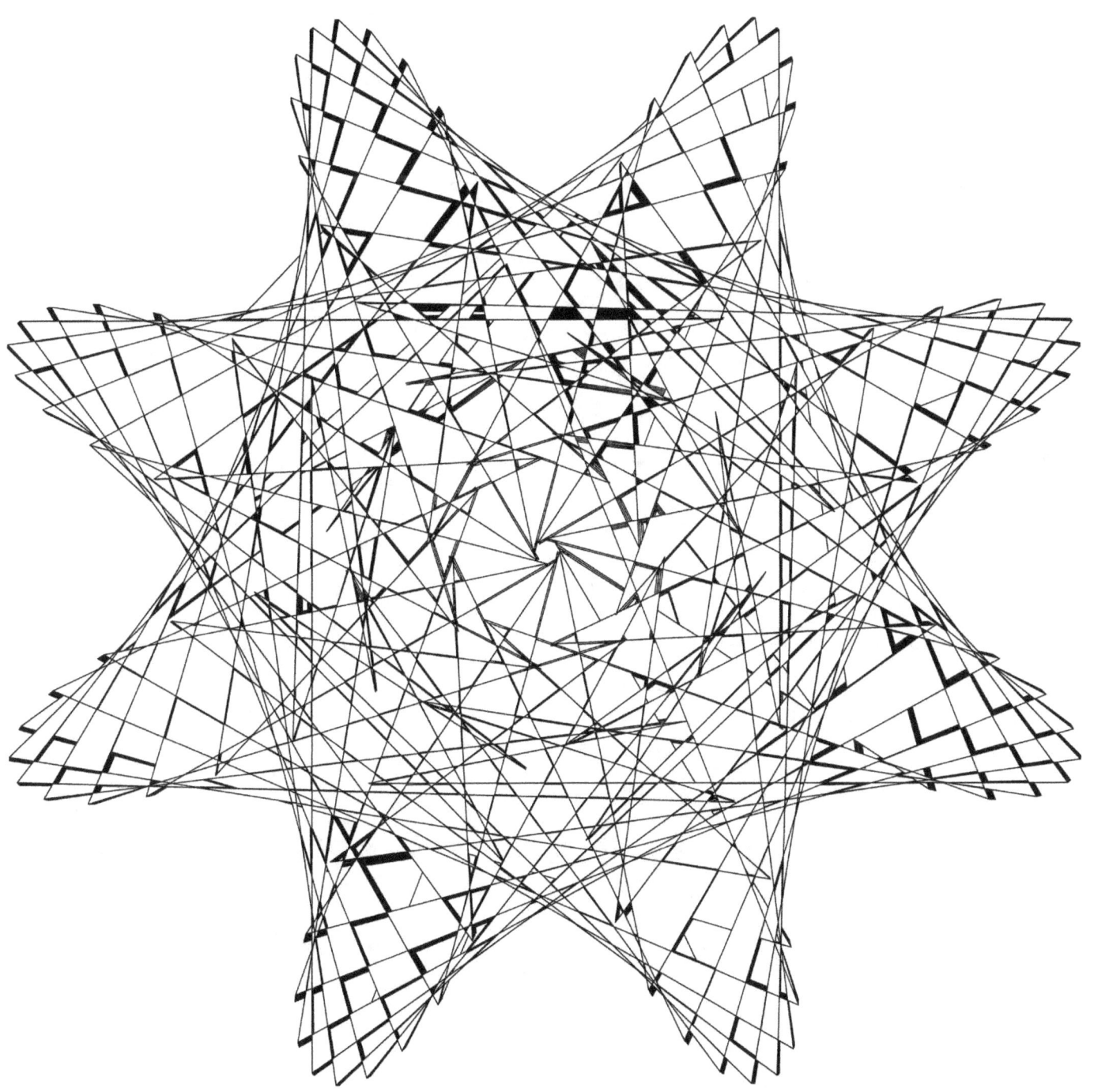

For more of my data adventures and math artwork, kindly visit me at aRtVerse (art-verse.com)!

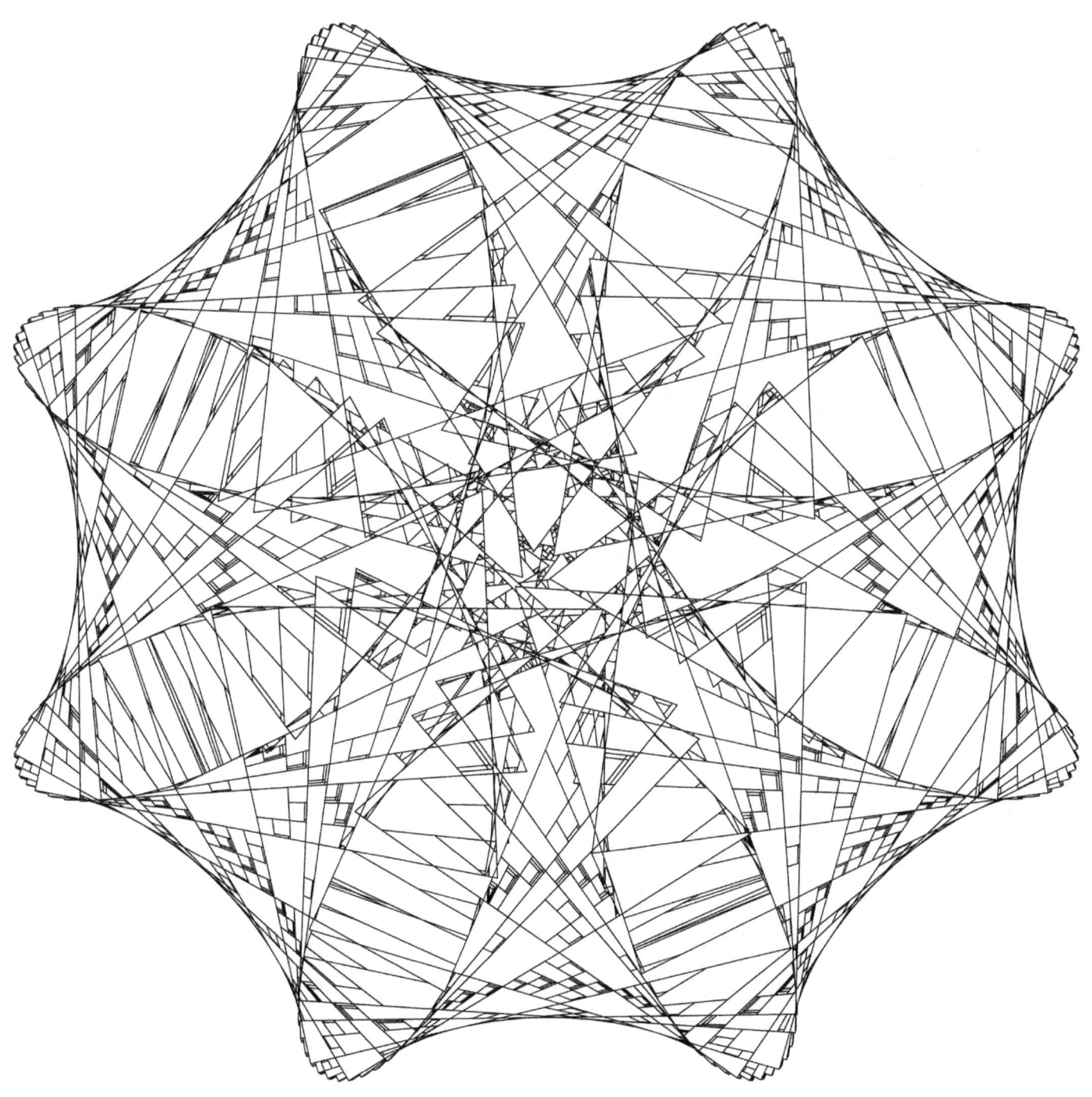

For more of my data adventures and math artwork, kindly visit me at aRtVerse (art-verse.com)!

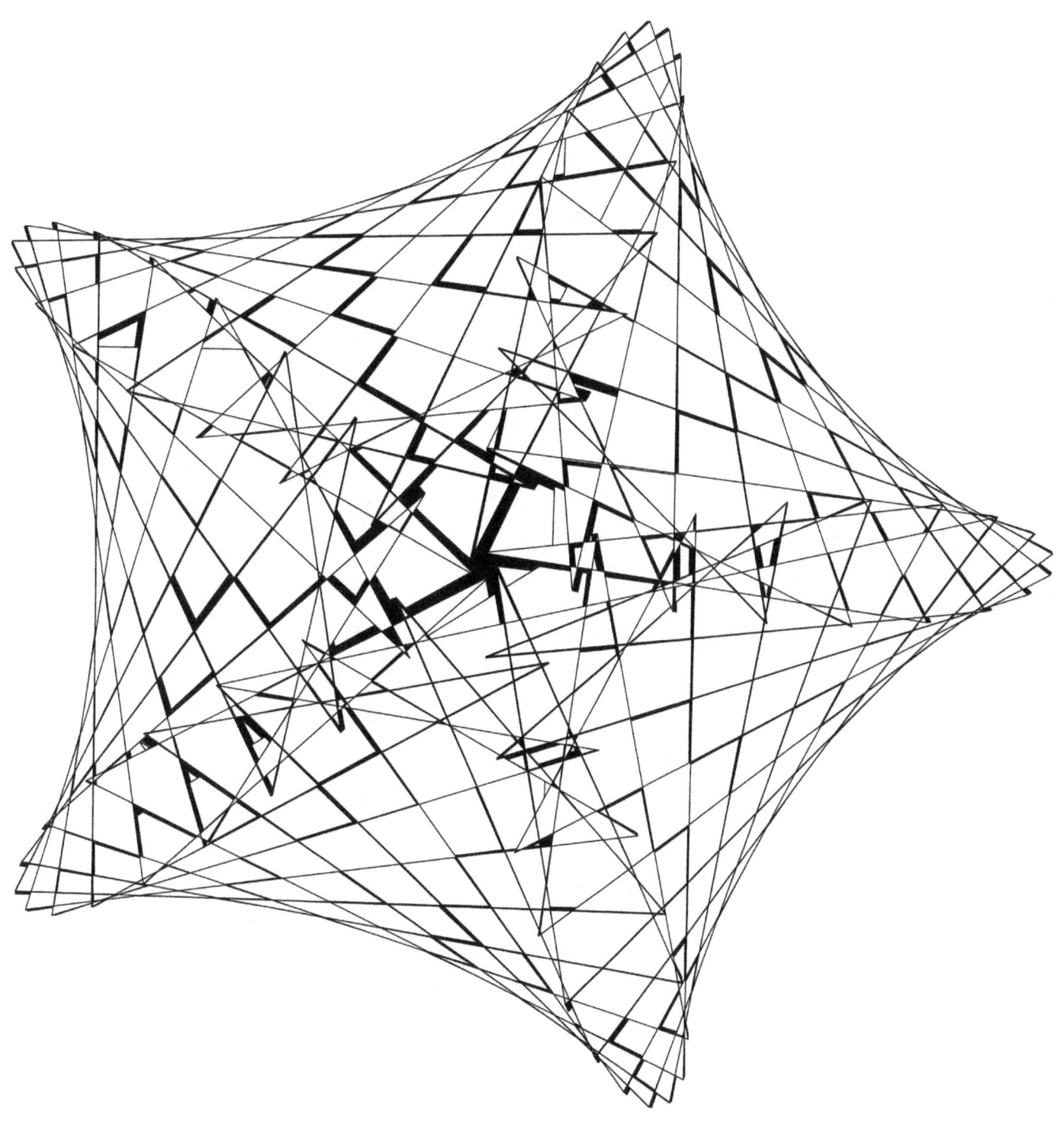

For more of my data adventures and math artwork, kindly visit me at aRtVerse (art-verse.com)!

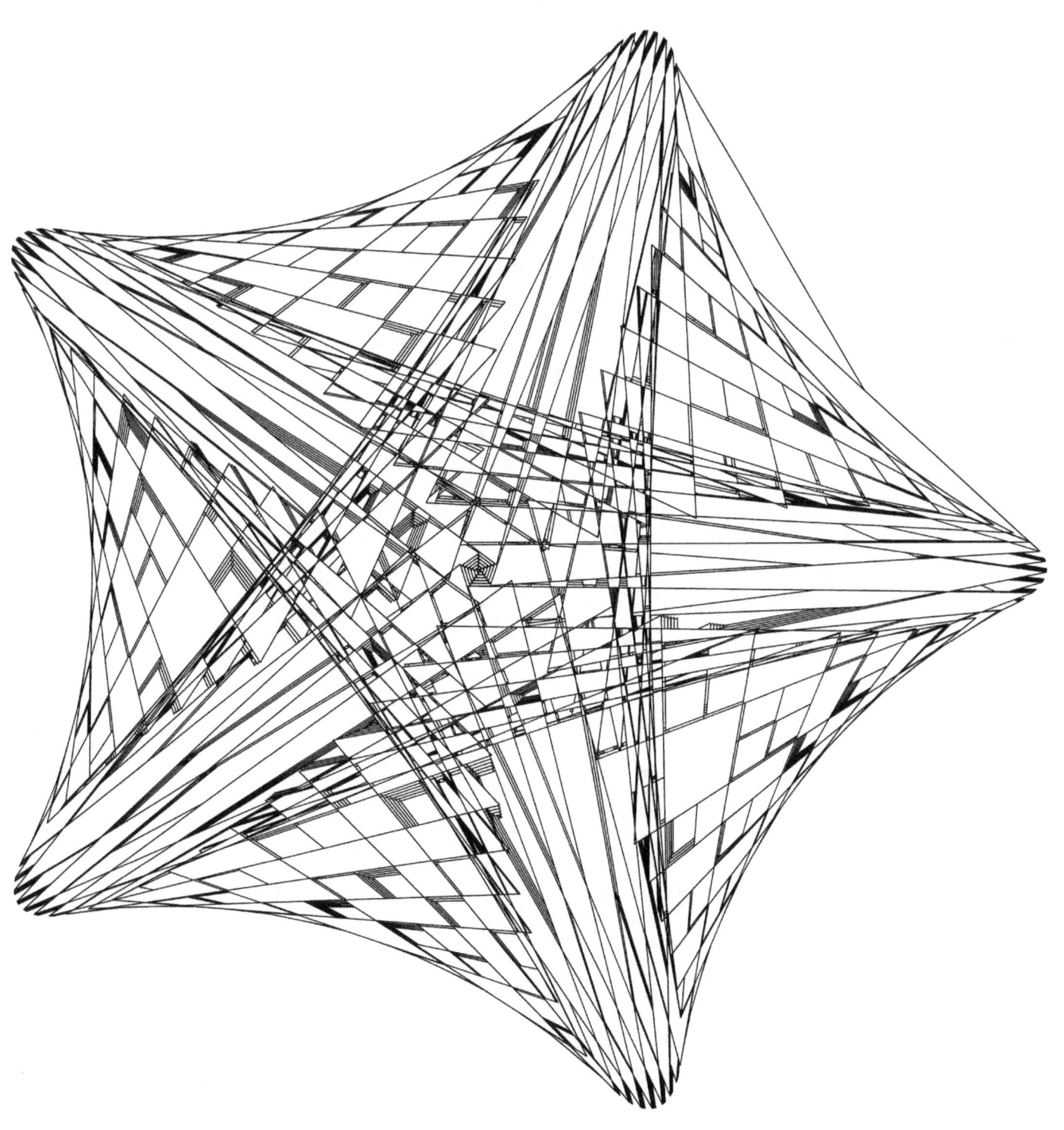

73 | MAURER ROSE ABSTRACTION CHALLENGE

For more of my data adventures and math artwork, kindly visit me at aRtVerse (art-verse.com)!

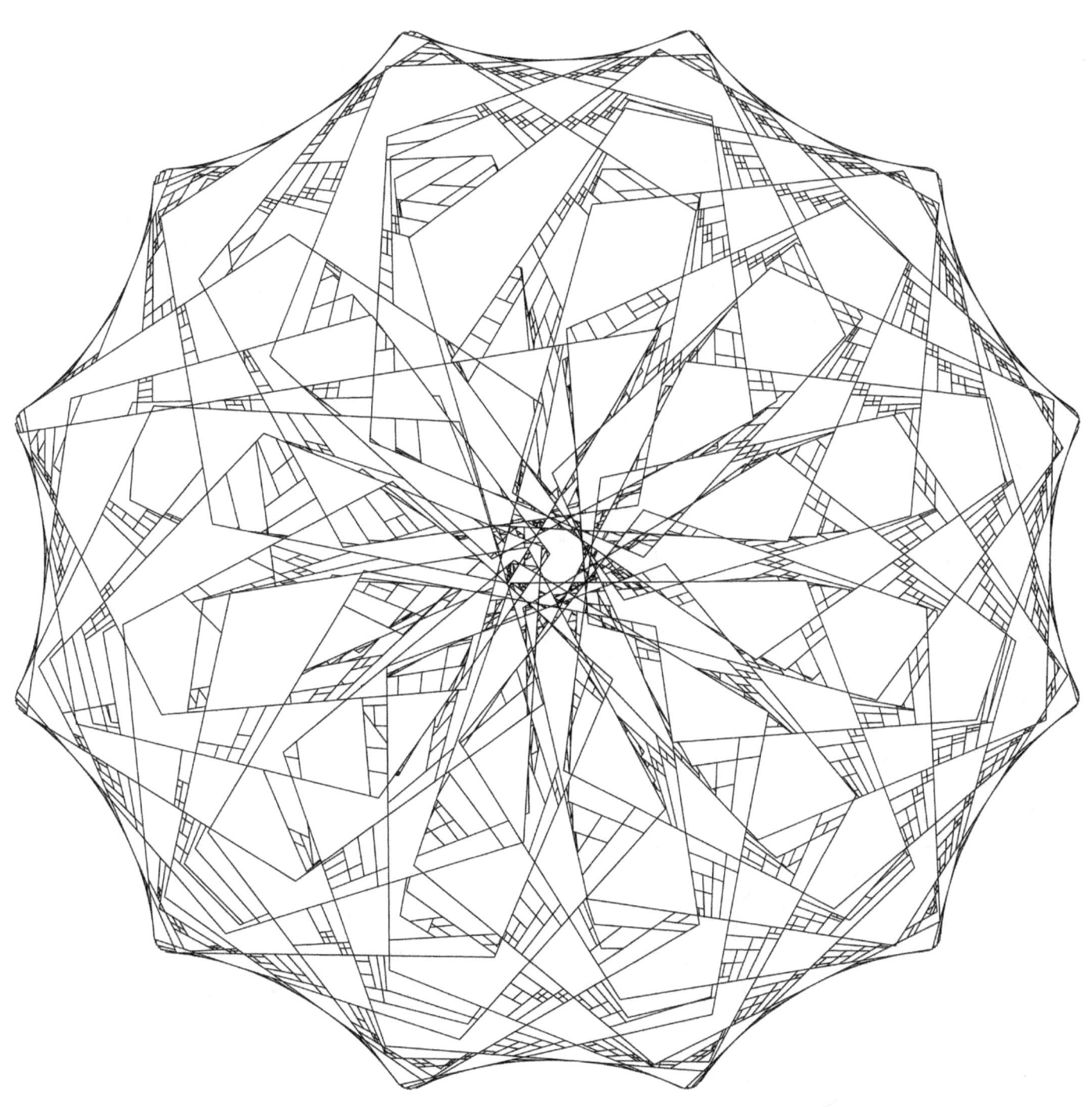

For more of my data adventures and math artwork, kindly visit me at aRtVerse (art-verse.com)!

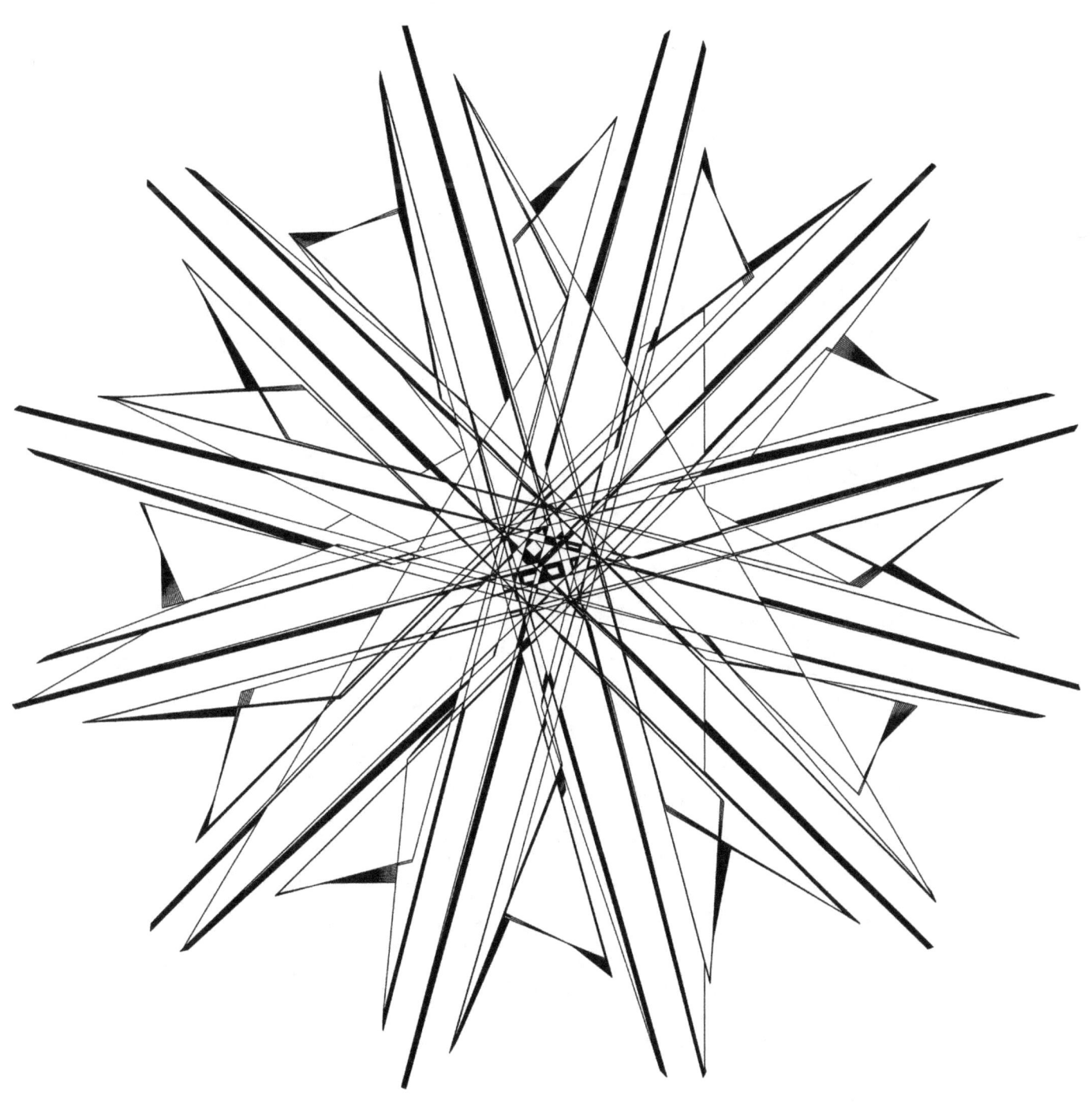

For more of my data adventures and math artwork, kindly visit me at aRtVerse (art-verse.com)!

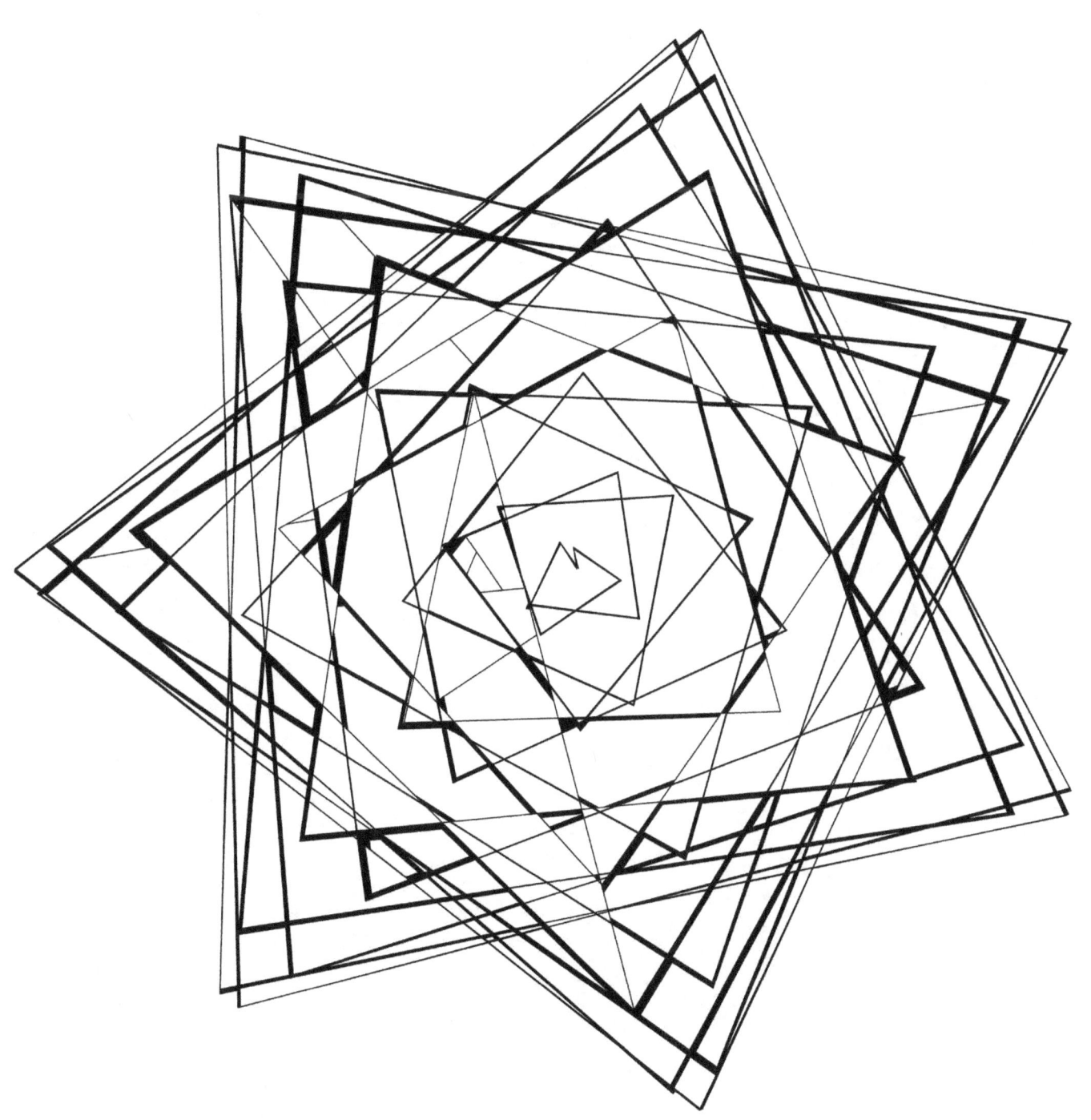

For more of my data adventures and math artwork, kindly visit me at aRtVerse (art-verse.com)!

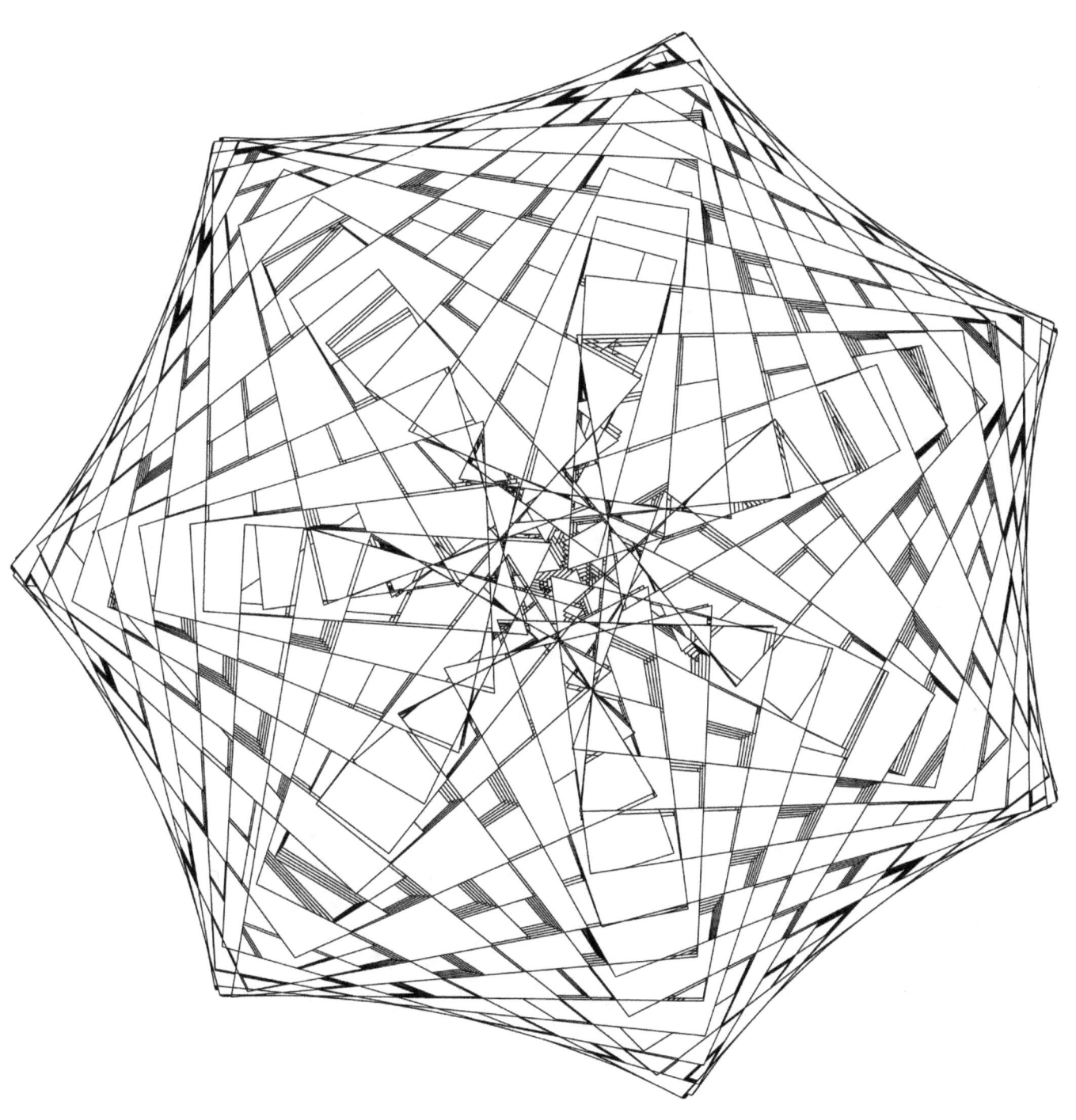

For more of my data adventures and math artwork, kindly visit me at aRtVerse (art-verse.com)!

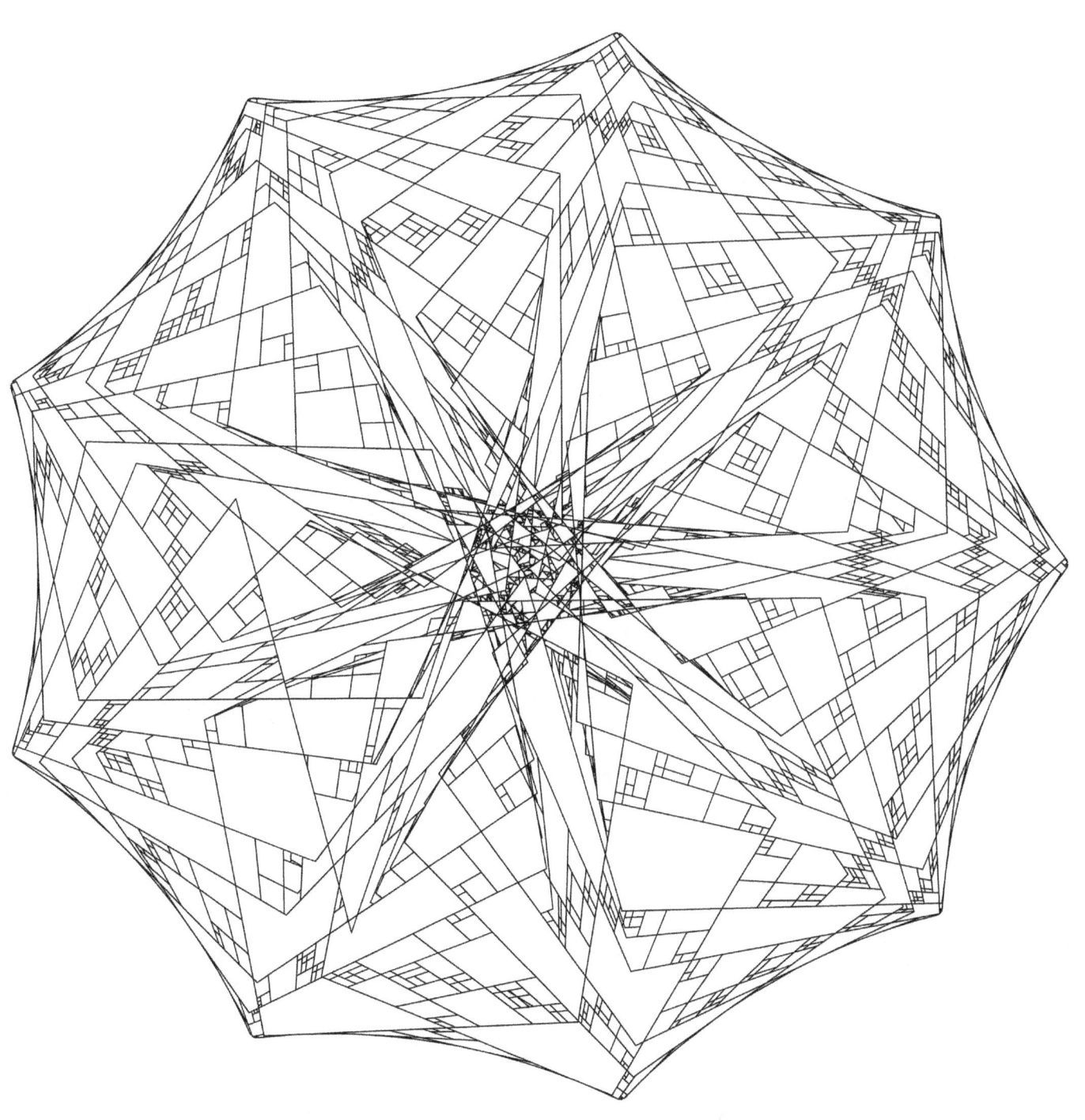

For more of my data adventures and math artwork, kindly visit me at aRtVerse (art-verse.com)!

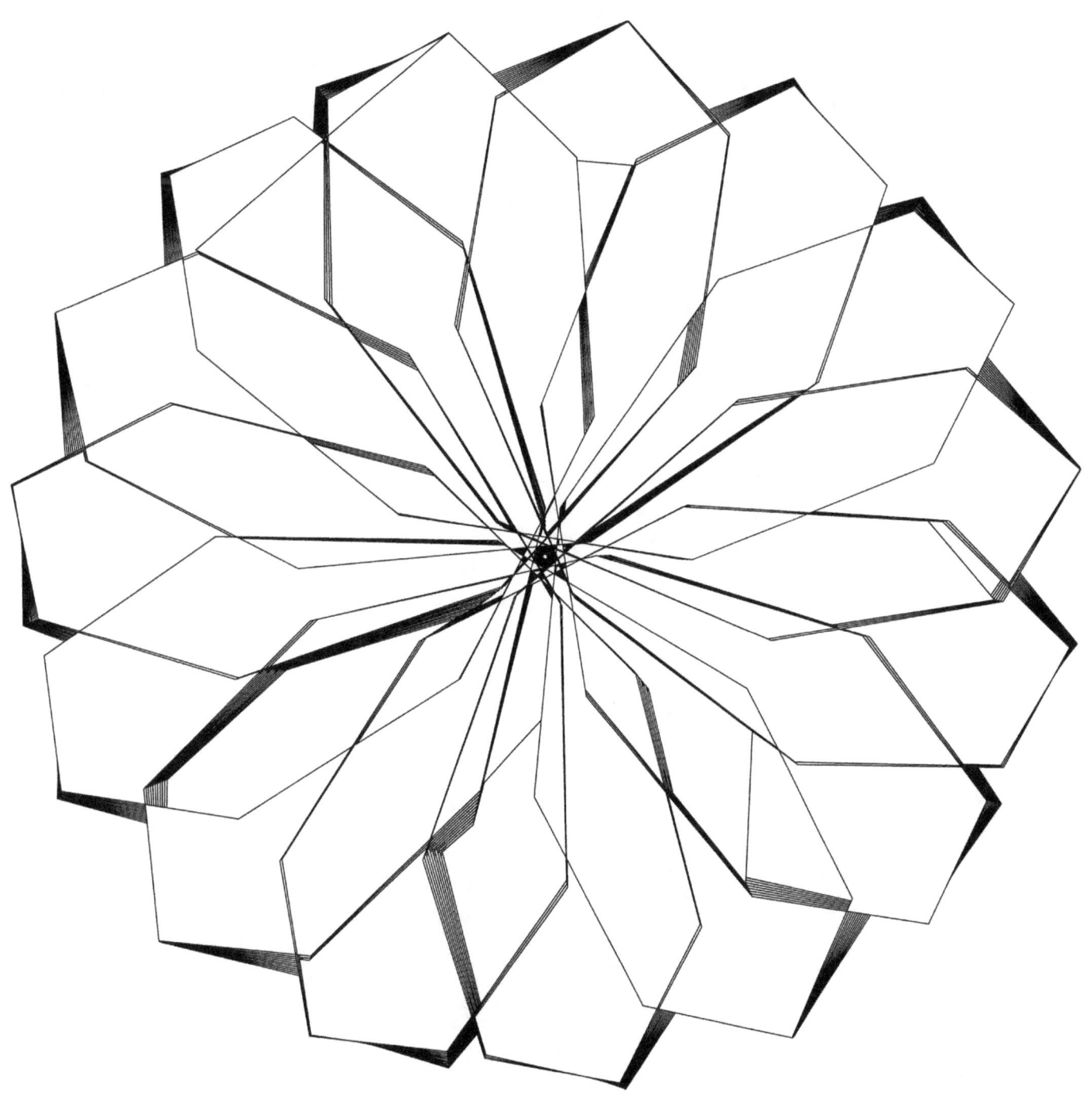

For more of my data adventures and math artwork, kindly visit me at aRtVerse (art-verse.com)!

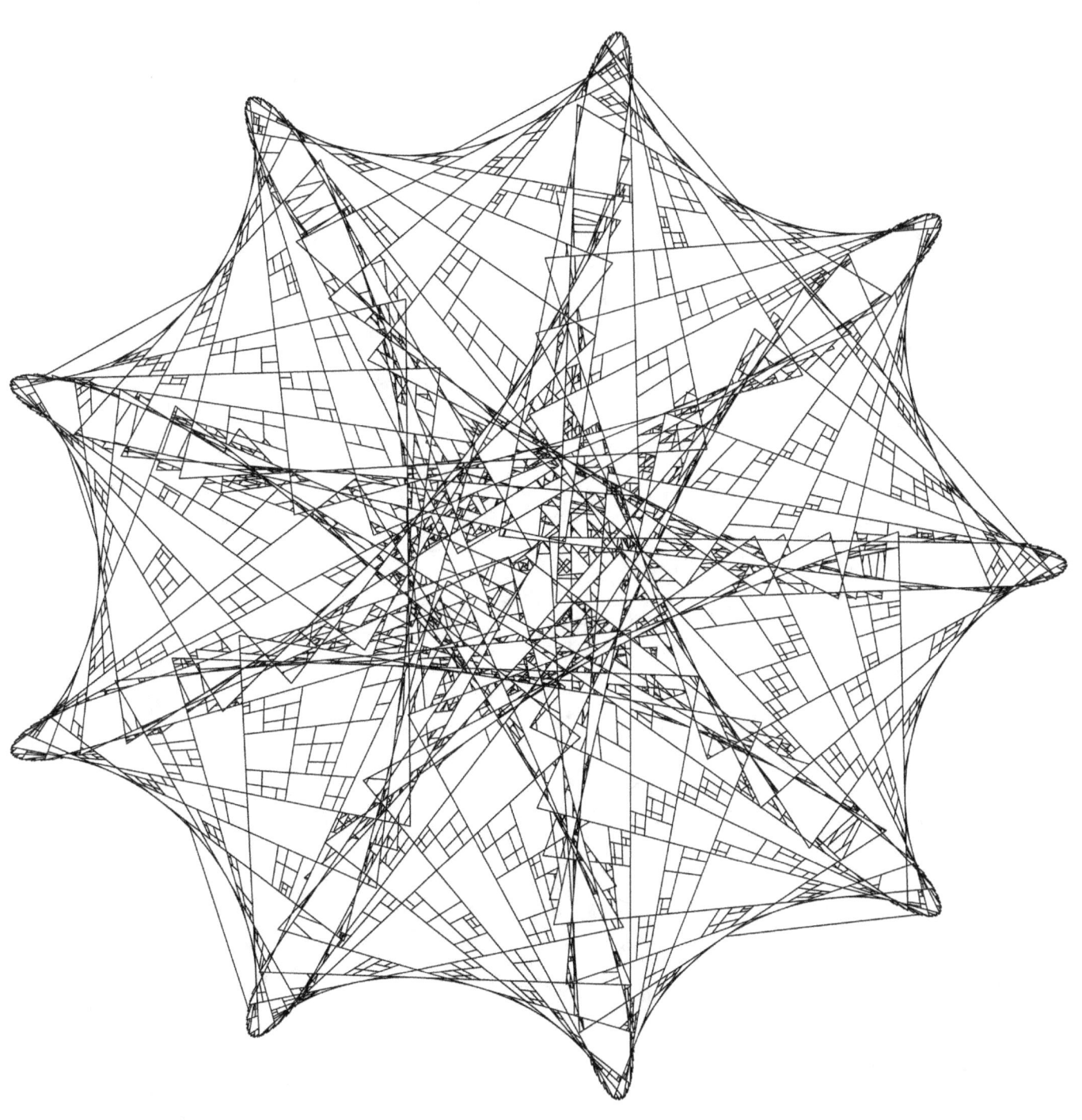

For more of my data adventures and math artwork, kindly visit me at aRtVerse (art-verse.com)!

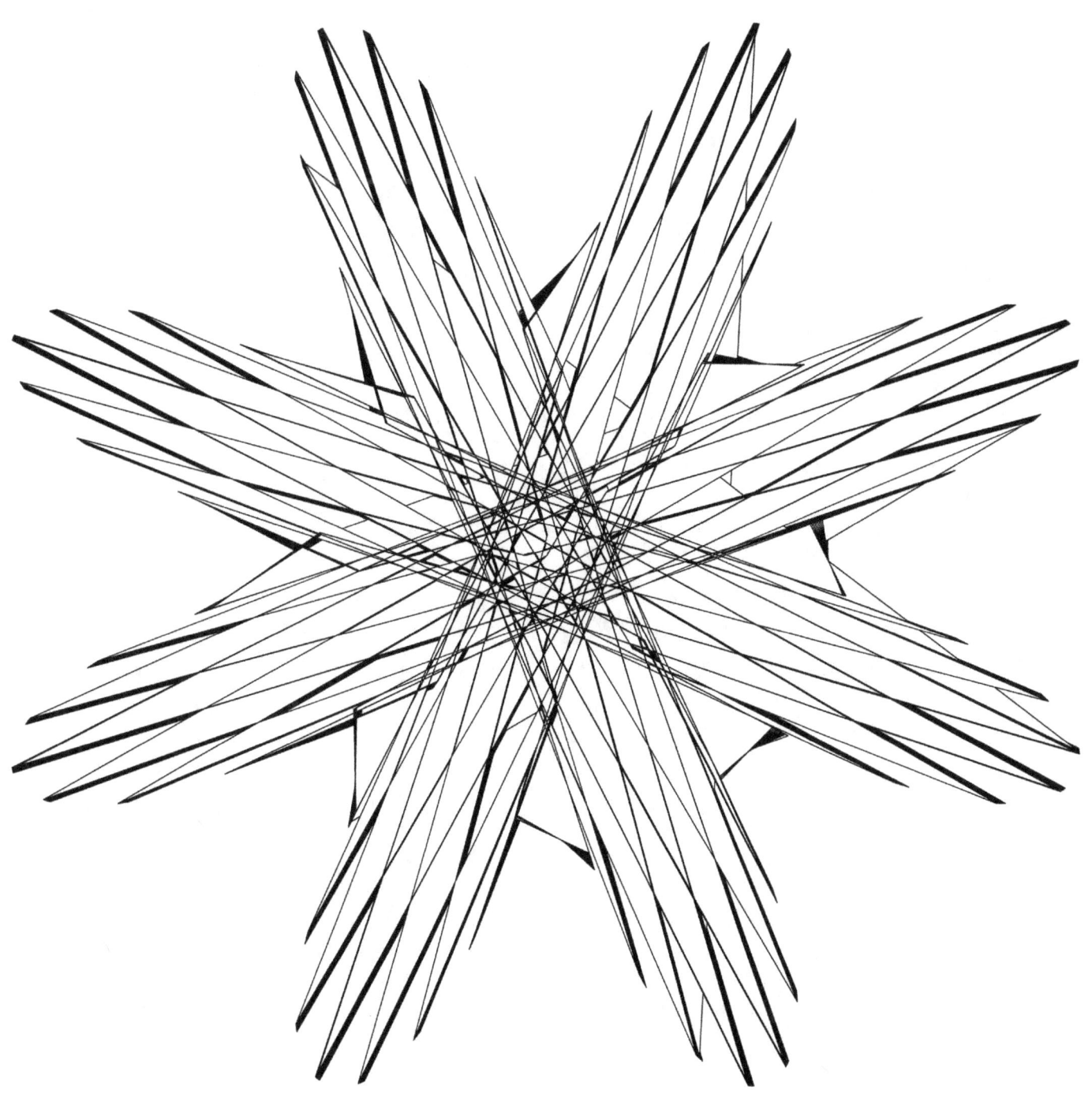

For more of my data adventures and math artwork, kindly visit me at aRtVerse (art-verse.com)!

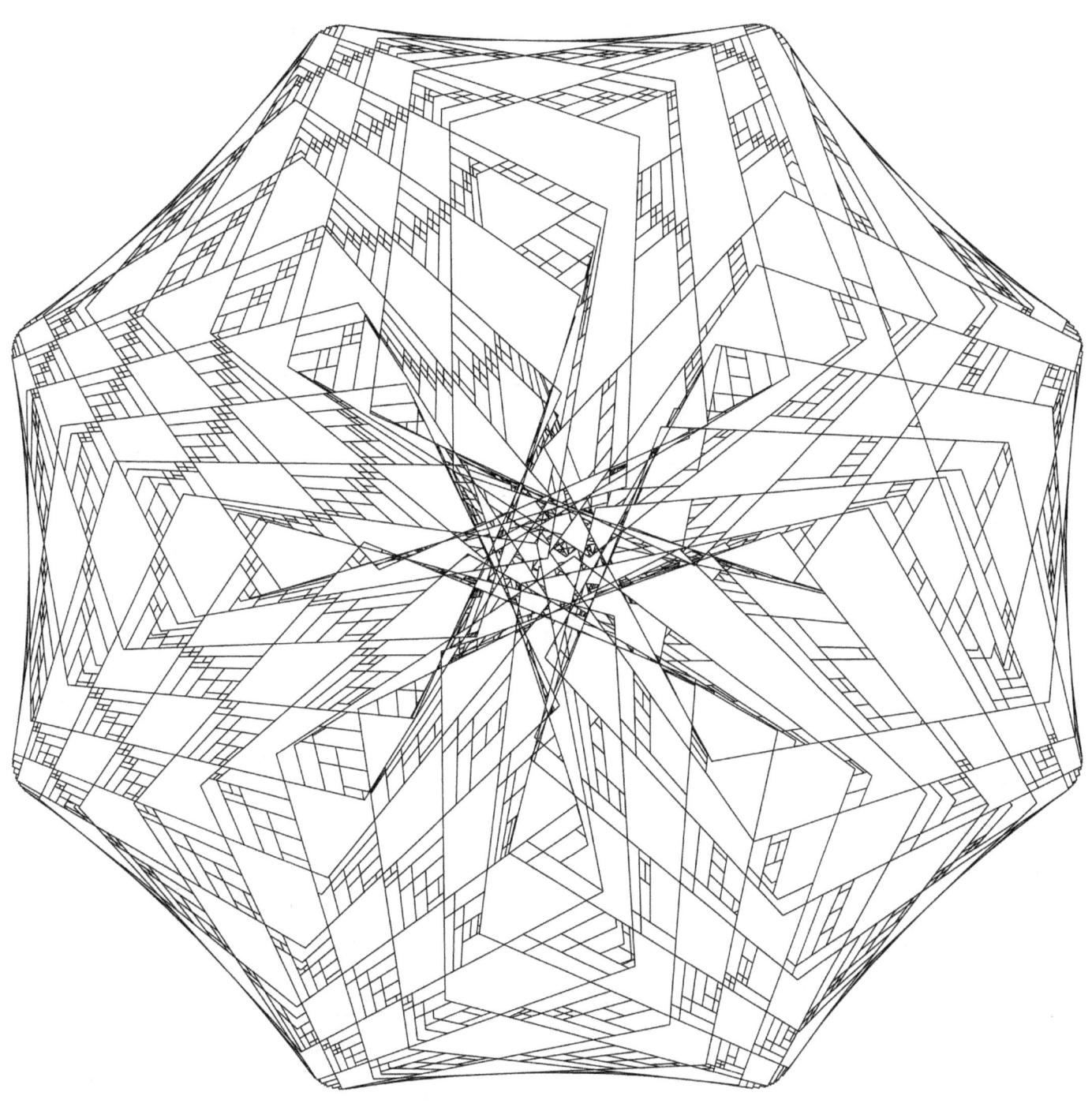

For more of my data adventures and math artwork, kindly visit me at aRtVerse (art-verse.com)!

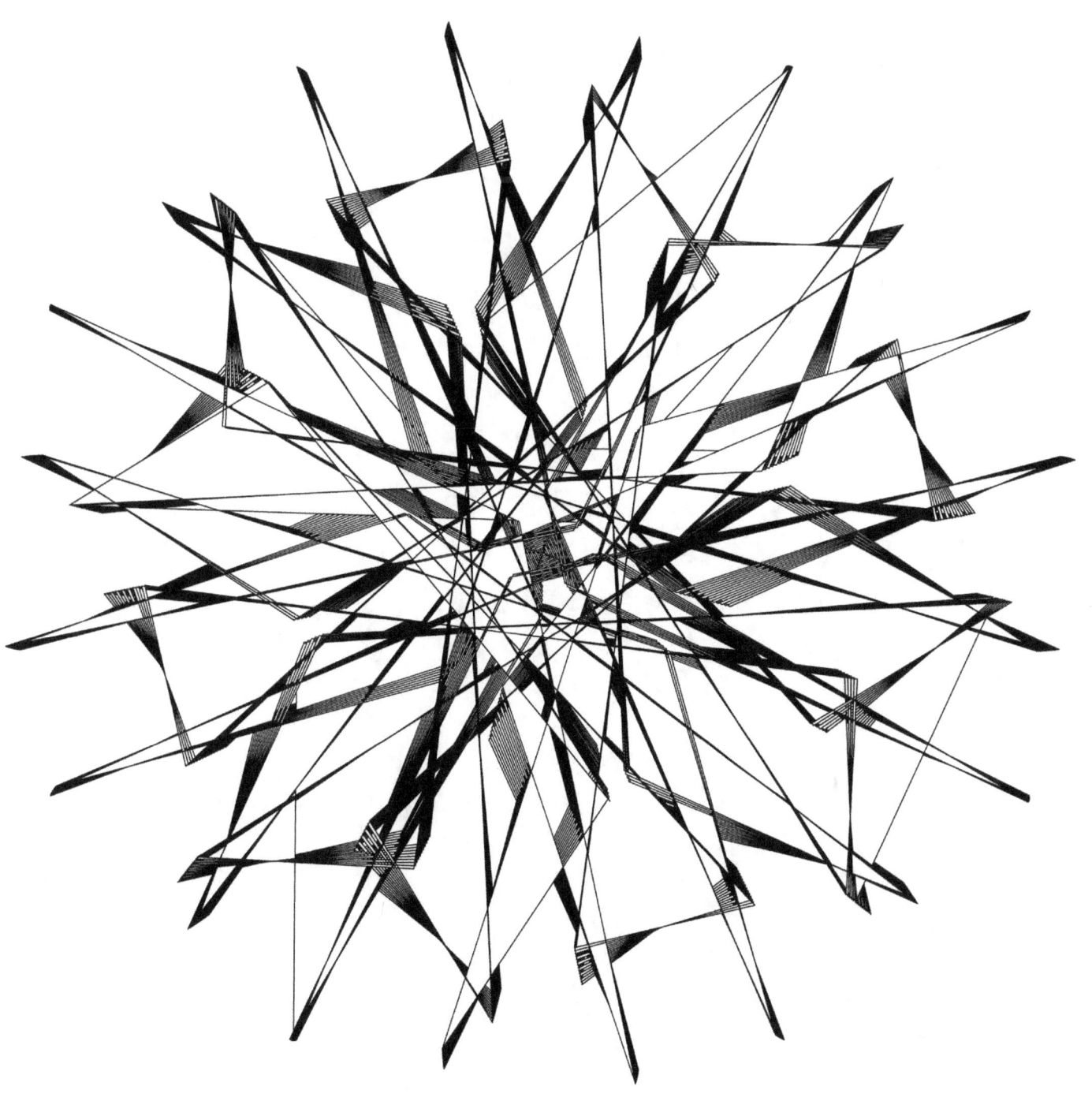

93 | MAURER ROSE ABSTRACTION CHALLENGE

For more of my data adventures and math artwork, kindly visit me at aRtVerse (art-verse.com)!

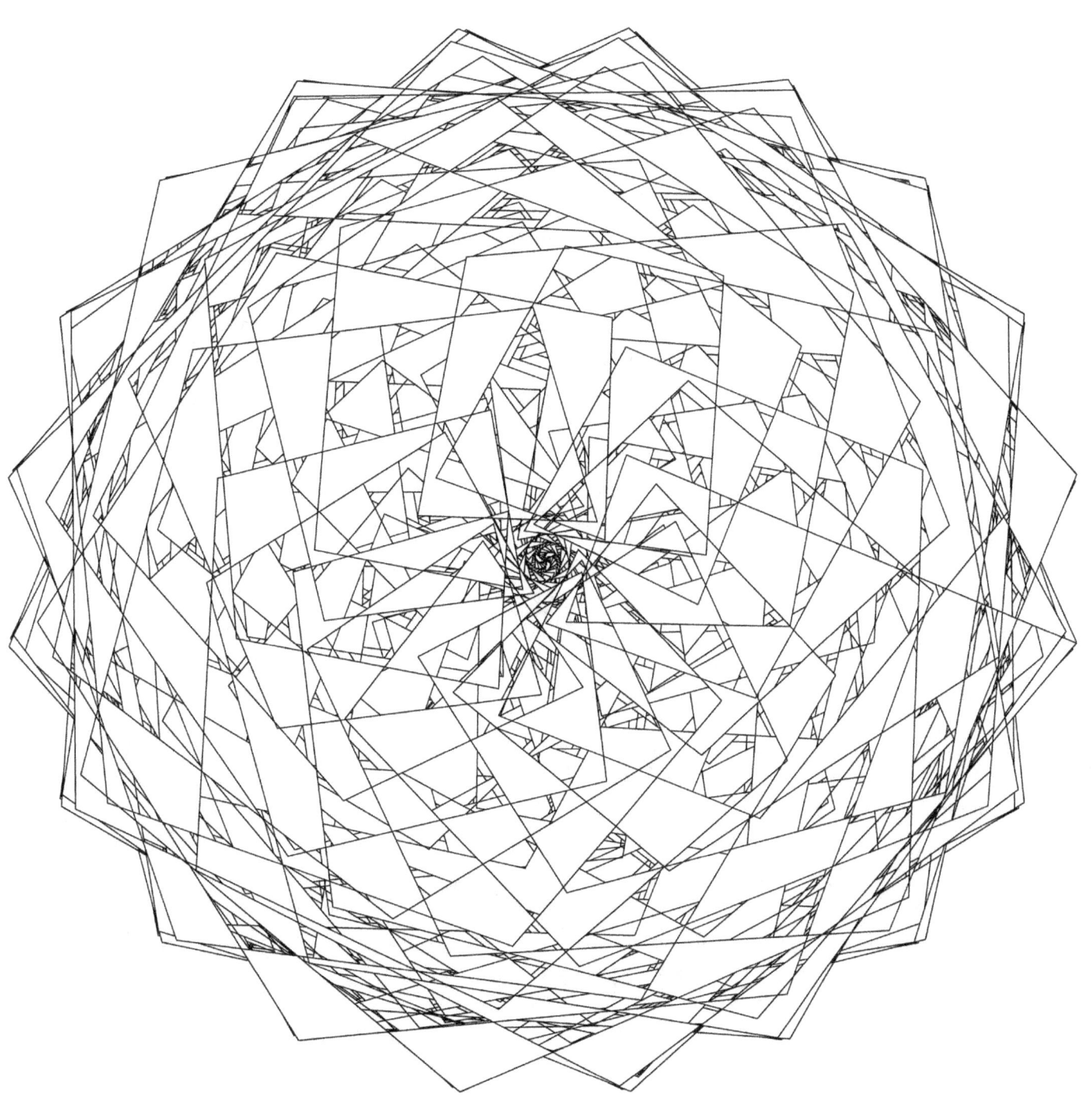

For more of my data adventures and math artwork, kindly visit me at aRtVerse (art-verse.com)!

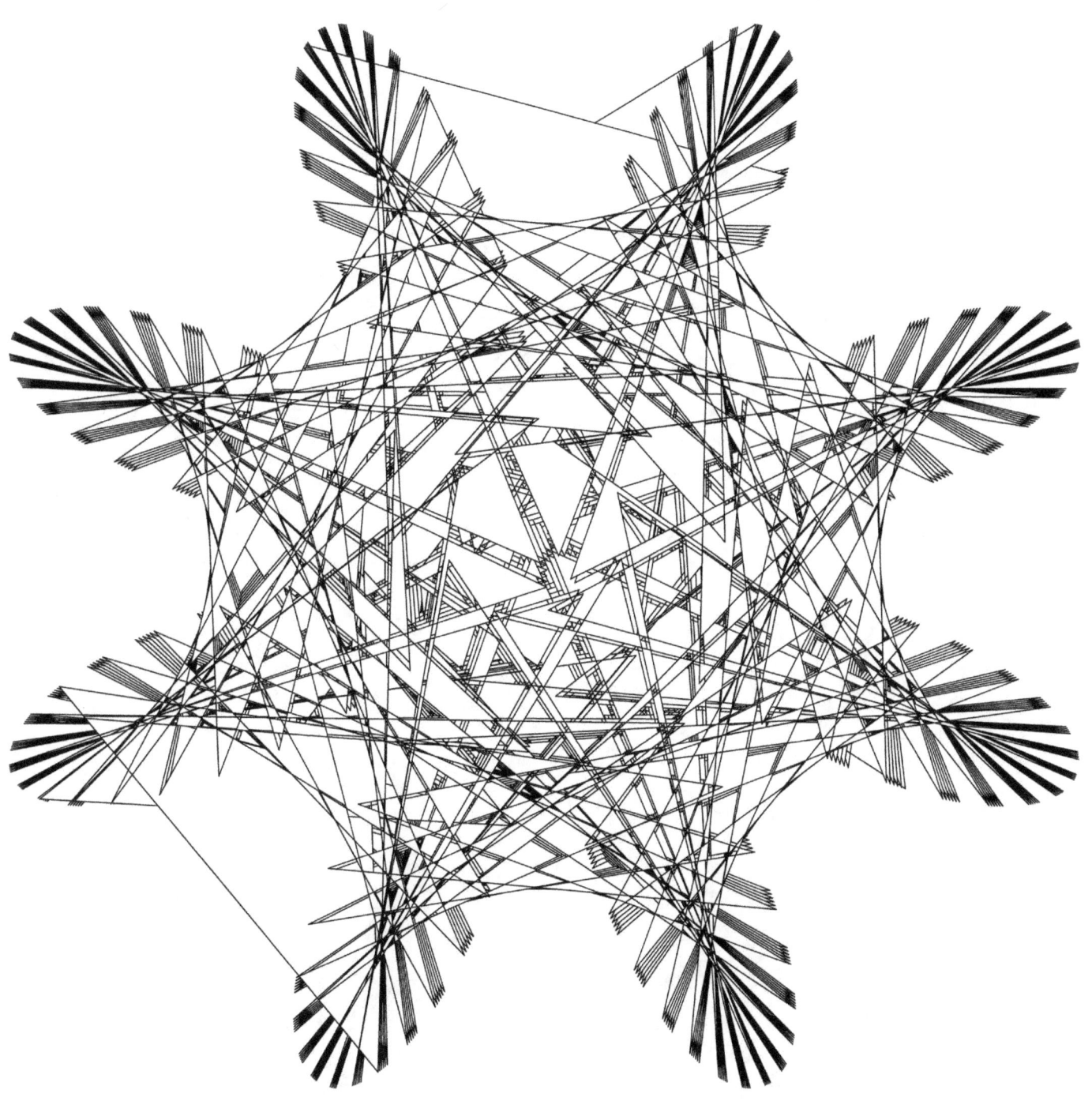

For more of my data adventures and math artwork, kindly visit me at aRtVerse (art-verse.com)!

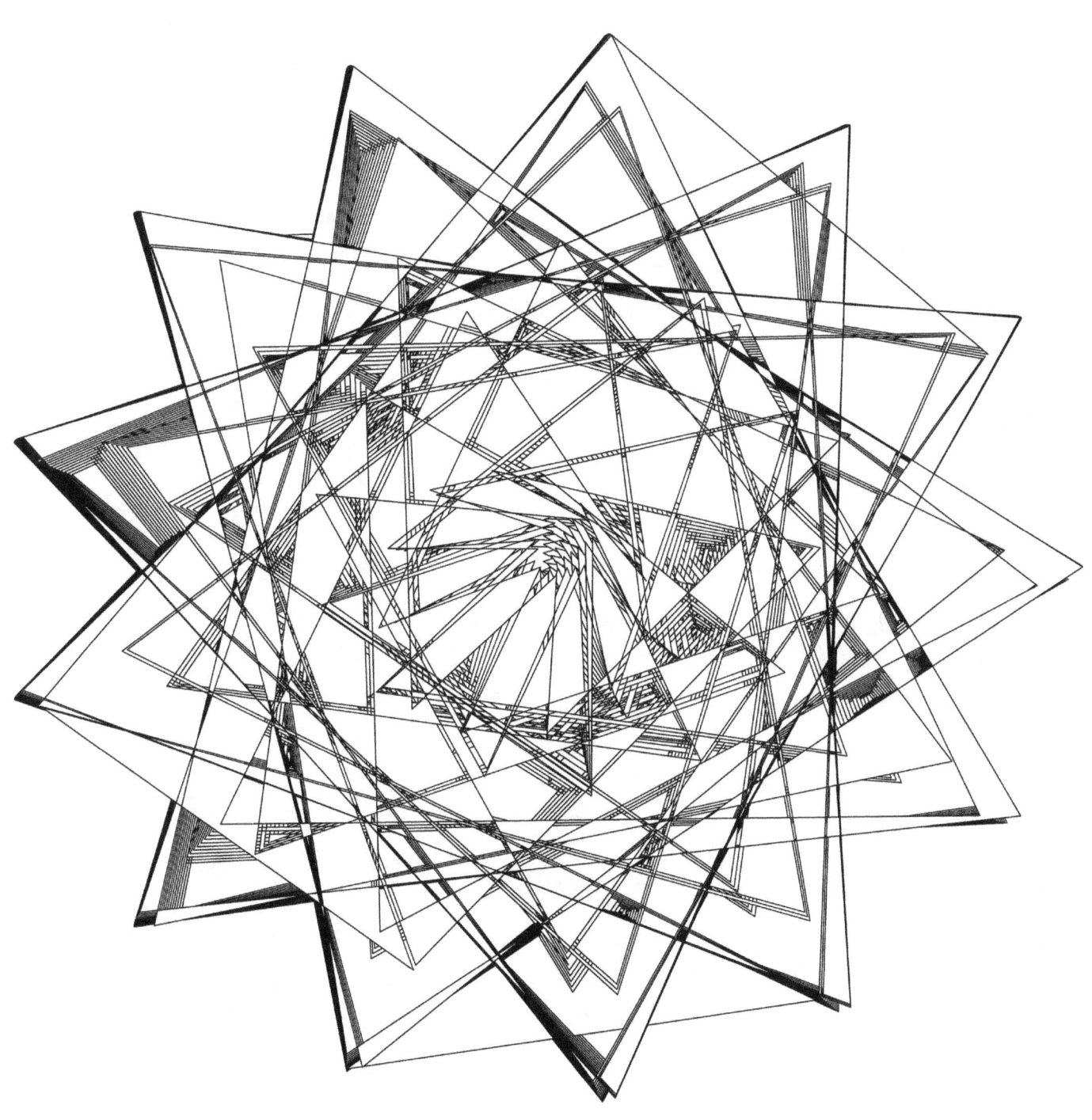

For more of my data adventures and math artwork, kindly visit me at aRtVerse (art-verse.com)!

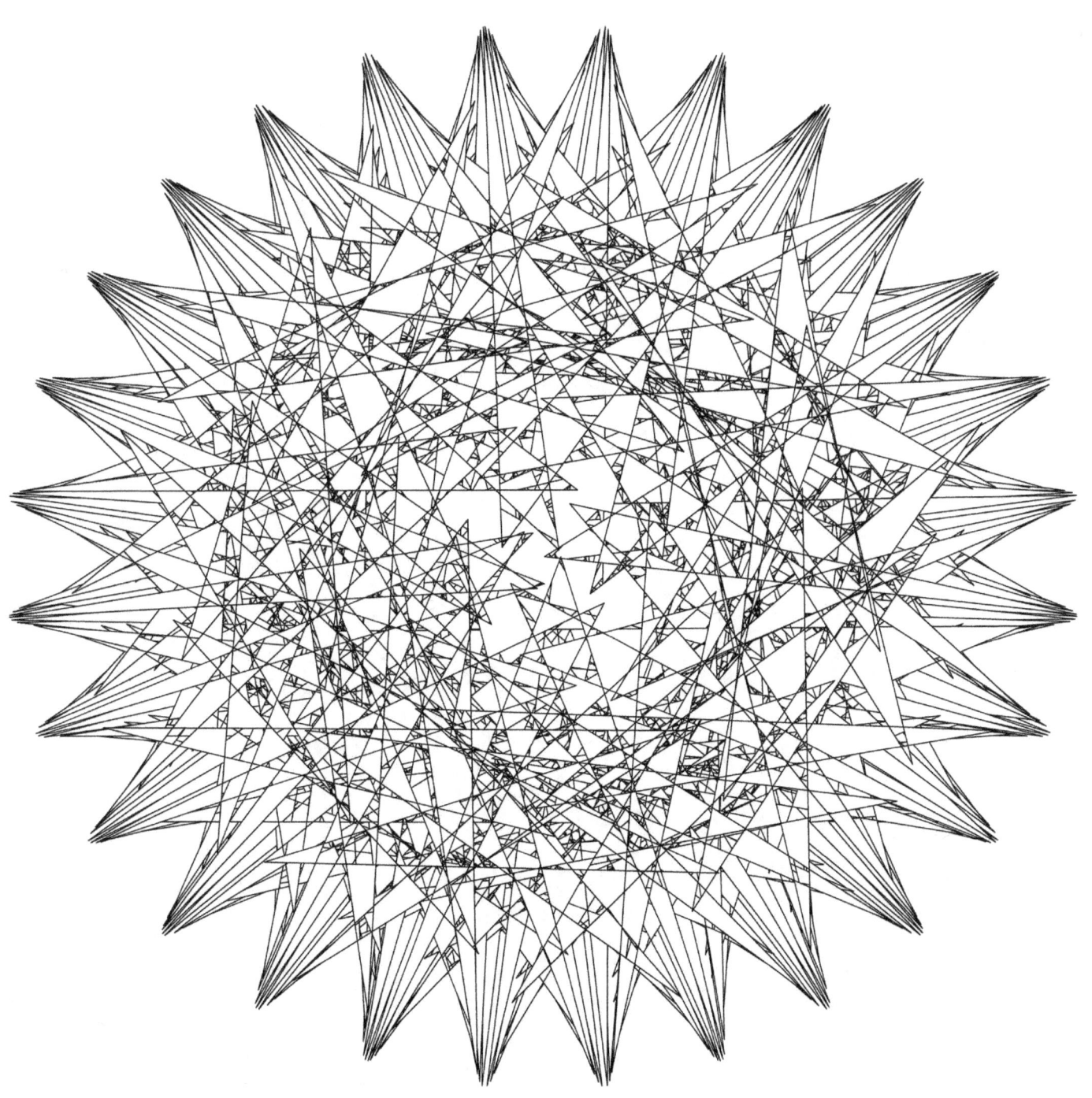

101 | MAURER ROSE ABSTRACTION CHALLENGE

For more of my data adventures and math artwork, kindly visit me at aRtVerse (art-verse.com)!

ABOUT THE AUTHOR

Dr Tanzelle Oberholster

Scientist | Writer | Artist | Pathfinder

I am formally educated in Molecular Biology with specialization in Genetics, Biotechnology and Microbiology. I write and post on my website (art-verse.com) where I share my art, my research, my ideas and my writing. This is an ongoing experiment with no rigid expectations, with loads of flexibility and plenty of adjustments as I go.

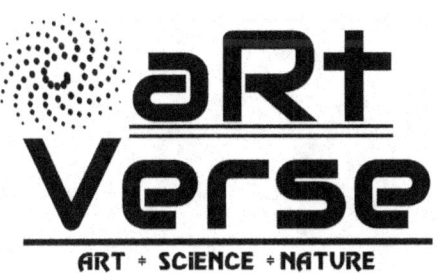

www.ingramcontent.com/pod-product-compliance
Lightning Source LLC
Chambersburg PA
CBHW082017230526
45466CB00022B/2428